100

THINGS TO DO IN

ESTES PARK

BEFORE YOU

DIE

100

THINGS TO DO IN
ESTES PARK
BEFORE YOU
DIE

• •

DAWN Y. WILSON

REEDY PRESS

Library of Congress Control Number: 2022950422

ISBN: 9781681064413

Design by Jill Halpin

All photos are by the author unless otherwise noted.
Cover image provided by Dawn Y. Wilson.

Printed in the United States of America
23 24 25 26 27   5 4 3 2 1

DEDICATION

To Clown, the palomino paint horse I rode during my first visit to Colorado in 1997, for teaching me about the ruggedness of Colorado and reminding me to always hold on for this amazing ride in the Rocky Mountains.

CONTENTS

● ●

● ●

Sports and Recreation

• •

• •

Culture and History

• •

Shopping and Fashion

• •

PREFACE

Clown was the palomino paint horse I rode out of Moraine Park Stables in Rocky Mountain National Park, which borders Estes Park to the south, west, and north, on my first visit to Colorado in July 1997. I came to Colorado that summer on a solo trip to tour a school I was considering for a graduate program. It was my first trip to the Centennial State, and, like many people who wind up here, it didn't take long for me to fall in love with this rugged country.

Clown, an older horse, frequently dragged his hooves across the numerous rocks on the trails and tripped during the four-hour ride. About three hours into the ride, he had enough and stumbled on yet another rock, causing me to slide off the saddle. I hit the ground hard and wound up with a bruise the size of a football on my hip that was visible for at least a month. Thankfully, that was the only thing that happened.

As soon as I returned home to New Jersey, all I could talk about was my visit to Colorado, the ride I took, the scenery I saw, and the crispness of the air. I knew I would someday live there.

I didn't go to graduate school in Colorado, opting to stay closer to home instead and finishing my master's degree at Temple University in Philadelphia.

Within two months of graduation, I had my house on the market and broke the news to my family that I was moving west. By September 30, 2002, I had the car packed and hit the road on a three-day trip to my new home in northern Colorado.

• •

Although I have missed friends, family, the Jersey Shore, and the food in New Jersey, I have found a home in Colorado. I have lived in Fort Collins, Arvada, Broomfield, and Loveland, but none of them have compared to living in Estes Park. This mountain town is home to about 6,500 people in the winter and expands to more than 11,000 in the summer with close to 4.5 million people passing through the gates of Rocky Mountain National Park each year. Most of those people use Estes Park as their basecamp.

After traveling in an RV for a year and a half, I found a marketing job in Estes Park and settled there. It took a little time to get used to living in the mountains: things cost a little more, wearing skirts went out the window for lack of practicality, and stopping at Walmart for a few things became a minimum three-hour journey. But now you would have to drag me kicking and screaming to change it.

I have had elk calves born outside my front door. Elk occasionally feed on the leaves of the aspen trees near my front steps, preventing me from leaving my home. I hear bugling on fall nights as the bull elk try to attract the attention of the cows. I can see moose in the morning, work all day at my desk, and watch the sun set behind an alpine lake. Even after being here since 2016, there are still dozens of trails I haven't yet completed.

• •

But in this time, I have written for two local newspapers, photographed wildlife and landscapes on more days than not throughout the year, and met many wonderful people—locals and travelers—who also enjoy the mountain lifestyle.

Estes Park offers a wide variety of activities for kicking back and relaxing or for being as active as you want to be. There are many options for the family visiting for the first time or the outdoor enthusiast who needs a break from the adventures.

Wild animals roam throughout the region. Remember to be respectful of wildlife and do not feed or chase them. When photographing wildlife, leave room and use a zoom.

Estes Park sits at 7,522 feet and everything in the area goes up from there. This elevation means Estes Park rarely gets into the upper 80s in summer and often drops below freezing in the depths of winter. Nights can be 30 to 40 degrees cooler than during the day, and temperatures along Trail Ridge Road can be 10 to 20 degrees cooler than in town.

Visitation in Rocky Mountain National Park has grown by almost 50 percent since 2012. To help curb the issues caused by such high numbers of visitors—the park was the fifth-most visited national park in 2021 with 4.43 million people entering its gates—park management implemented a timed-entry reservation system in 2020.

• •

This system has caused some confusion since its implementation, and although the communication has improved, the details can be murky. The specifics and dates for the reservation system change slightly each year so visit nps.gov/romo/planyourvisit/timed-entry-permit-system.htm for the latest information.

For additional information, contact Visit Estes Park (visitestespark.com), Estes Park Chamber of Commerce (esteschamber.org), Rocky Mountain National Park (nps.gov/romo), or the Town of Estes Park (estespark.colorado.gov).

I know you will find this book helpful, informative, and entertaining. Enjoy your visit to Estes Park and the Rocky Mountains.

Cheers,
Dawn Wilson
dawnwilsonphotography.com

• •

ACKNOWLEDGMENTS

This book represents more than two decades of exploring Colorado, Estes Park, and Rocky Mountain National Park. Although I estimate I have hiked more than 250 miles of trails in the park, I also enjoy learning about the region's history, unique characters, and abundant wildlife that make this area such a special place. I know I cannot list everyone, but these are just a few of the many people who have helped me learn more about this amazing mountain town. Thank you to the following people who have shared their knowledge, tips, and advice over the years: David Bates, Mary Davis, Heather Drees, Sherrie Duris, Richard Hahn, Annie Hanson, Gary and Kris Hazelton, Marsha Hobert, Rick Martinez, Bob and Cindy Maynard, David Neils, James Pickering, Scott Rashid, Wendy Rigby, Vic Schendel, Erik Stensland, Deena Sveinsson, staff at Visit Estes Park, and all of the countless photographers, guides, writers, historians, library staff, park staff, and random locals and visitors who shared their bits of info over the years.

A special thank you goes out to my mom and dad for always encouraging me to follow my passions and not give up.

A special thank you to Aeric Luciano for agreeing to move to Colorado all those years ago. I know you will never be able to see this, but your insight, passion, and love for the outdoors is with me every single day.

• •

And to Richard Barberot, thank you for sharing this journey with me. I know Estes Park wasn't your first choice, but I thank you from the bottom of my heart for putting up with all the extra dog walks and early morning alarms and for patiently waiting for me after a "I won't be long" note. There are many more journeys out there to be made! Let's go!

FOOD AND DRINK

INDULGE YOURSELF
WITH CHERRY PIE, COLORADO STYLE

Most people don't think of cherries as a mountain-grown food, but Colorado Cherry Company has built a following as THE source of the best cherry pies in the region. Since co-owner Anthony Lehnert's grandmother started baking pies in the 1920s, this fourth-generation family continues the tradition of home-baked pies. Beyond cherry, Lehnert and his wife, Kristi, also offer apple, blueberry, cherry streusel, mixed berry, blackberry, strawberry rhubarb, and the popular favorite, bourbon caramel apple pies. Colorado Cherry Company has a wide selection of other products made with cherries, including coffee, hot sauce, mustard, fruit spreads, preserves, and fruit juices. Their Lyons location on US Highway 36 in the St. Vrain Canyon also has a café and bakery that serves lunch and dinner with delicious bison pot pies on the menu.

Inside the Stanley Hotel
333 Wonderview Ave., 970-577-4000

US Hwy. 36/St. Vrain Canyon
12311 N St. Vrain Rd., Lyons, 888-526-6535

US Hwy. 34/Big Thompson Canyon
1024 US 34, Loveland, 970-667-4141

coloradocherrycompany.com

BIKE THROUGH TOWN
ON A BREWERY TOUR

Estes Park is home to five craft breweries, and since most of them are within biking, or even walking, distance of each other, a brewery tour makes a lot of sense. An additional bonus: Colorado has an average of 300 days of sunshine a year, perfect weather for pedaling around Estes Park. Stopping at Lumpy Ridge Brewing Company, Rock Cut Brewing Company, and The Barrel, this six-mile bike ride gets you a little exercise, some fresh air, and samples of the best microbrews in the mountains. Just a mile farther down the road is the Estes Park Brewery. Didn't bring a bike? Estes Park Mountain Shop rents bikes and several hotels, including the Ridgeline, offer free bikes for guests. Please remember to drink responsibly and check your rental agreement for any limitations on distance or destinations.

Estes Park Mountain Shop
2050 Big Thompson Ave., 970-586-6548
estesparkmountainshop.com

The Ridgeline Hotel
101 S St. Vrain Ave., 970-527-1500
ridgelinehotel.com

ENJOY A SLOW AFTERNOON WITH A GLASS OF WINE
AT SNOWY PEAKS WINERY

Snowy Peaks Winery is located on Moraine Avenue at one of the busiest corners in town. Why? The bulk of the traffic comes out of the south entrance from Rocky Mountain National Park and passes by this family-friendly winery. Instead of sitting in traffic, stop for a little downtime after a hike and enjoy a glass of award-winning, hand-crafted wine. While sitting on the front patio you will have breath-taking views of the Continental Divide. If you choose the back patio, you will be able to listen to the hypnotic sound of the Big Thompson River. If you can't decide or want to experiment, try the tasting flight of five samples of wines of your choice. Cheeses, handmade jellies, and other gourmet foods that pair well with wines are available for sale to eat with your wine selection or to take home. Open daily from 12 to 6:30 p.m.

292 Moraine Ave., 970-586-2099
snowypeakswinery.com

PACK A LUNCH AND FISHING POLE FOR A PICNIC
AT LAKE ESTES

Lake Estes has been the center of activity in Estes Park since the completion of the Olympus Dam created the lake in 1949. There are numerous picnic shelters around the lake at Wapiti Meadows, Cherokee Draw, Fisherman's Nook, and the Lake Estes Marina where anglers can have a picnic lunch while setting up a fishing pole to catch some of the trout with which the lake is stocked. Several local restaurants provide takeout options, including sandwiches from the Egg of Estes, Scratch Deli, and the Sandwich Mafia. There are also two Subway locations in downtown Estes Park that open early for those heading out for a day in the outdoors. There is a parking fee at all areas around Lake Estes except at Fisherman's Nook.

The Egg of Estes
393 E Elkhorn Ave., 970-586-1173
eggofestes.com

Scratch Deli
911 Moraine Ave., 970-586-8383

The Sandwich Mafia
100 Cleave St., 970-591-2400
sandwich-mafia.com

Subway (Stanley Village)
517 Big Thompson Ave., 970-577-7744

Subway (River Park Plaza)
184 E Elkhorn Ave., 970-586-5023

HOOK A BREW AND TASTY FISH FILET
AT LUMPY RIDGE BREWERY

Food trucks have become very popular in Estes Park during the summer months. Several vendors come into town, bringing with them hamburgers, Mexican fare, and barbecue. The best, as confirmed by the long line all day when in town, is On the Hook Fish and Chips. Hate waiting in line? On the Hook co-owners Hunter Anderson and Ocean Andrew have conveniently decided that Lumpy Ridge Brewing Company is the best location for their truck so while you wait for your freshly fried, line-caught, wild Alaskan cod, order a beer and have a seat on the patio. Extra bonus: Dogs are allowed on the patio with you. As a craft brewery, their selection of beers on tap regularly changes, but if it is available, try the Ogg's FM German Amber Lager. Enjoying a German beer on the deck with views of the Rocky Mountains will make you think you are sitting in a beer garden in the German Alps. You will have the added bonus of flaky, fried Alaskan cod to eat along with your beer. Check On the Hook's website for dates and times when their truck will be in Estes Park.

Lumpy Ridge Brewing
531 S St. Vrain Ave., 970-235-1752
lumpyridgebrewing.com

On the Hook Fish and Chips
307-316-4665
onthehookfishandchips.com

WARM UP YOUR BELLY WITH A LOCALLY DISTILLED WHISKEY
AT ESTES PARK'S FIRST LEGAL DISTILLERY

Sitting at 7,522 feet, Estes Park can have cold winters with strong winds. The cure for that winter chill? A shot of whiskey from Estes Park's first legal distillery. Elkins Distilling started as a small, craft distillery in 2016 by two unlikely men: an Earth sciences professor with a Ph.D. in geology and a self-proclaimed redneck from a dry town in a dry county in Alabama. They opened Estes Park's first legal distillery, using 100 percent Colorado-grown grains and water from Rocky Mountain National Park's watershed, and distilling every drop of the whiskey they served right on-site. An explosion and fire in early 2021 closed their main tasting room, but not to fret: a second location in downtown Estes Park offers a place to sip, purchase, and shop. Not a fan of whiskey? Try their apple flavor for a sweeter, less bitter option. Not into shots? Try a Vanilla Old Fashioned, made with Elkins Colorado Single Barrel Bourbon Whisky, Elkins Colorado Vanilla Cocktail Syrup, and a splash of juice from a fresh orange.

137 E Elkhorn Ave., 970-480-1848
Instagram: @elkinswhisky

FEED THE MALLARDS WHILE ENJOYING A LATTE
AT COFFEE ON THE ROCKS

Just outside the south entrance to Rocky Mountain National Park, Coffee on the Rocks is a popular spot to stop after a hike or for a jolt of caffeine before heading into the park. If hiking isn't in your plans, enjoy your coffee on their outdoor patio where for one dollar a cup, you can buy corn to feed the mallard ducks that make full use of the shop's pond. Thanks to an aerator, winter is particularly popular with the ducks because the pond water doesn't freeze. Looking for Hemingway's "clean, well-lighted place" to compose your novel? Join the other writers in the back of Coffee on the Rocks, where a large room with tables offers a great spot to work, read, write, or meet with friends over a coffee. The shop also sells teas, mochas, frappes, smoothies, breakfast, lunch, beer, and wine. If you like sweet lattes, try the Razz, a latte with white chocolate and raspberry. Open daily but hours change depending on the season.

510 Moraine Ave., 970-909-4836
coffeeontherocks.co

GET A TASTE OF SOUTHERN-STYLE BARBECUE
IN THE MOUNTAIN AIR

Although founder Dave Oehlman has since expanded his barbecue business to four locations along the Front Range, he started his award-winning barbecue right here in Estes Park. Smokin' Dave's BBQ & Brew rocks the best barbecue in northern Colorado. Never mind that mountain towns are not known for smoking great barbecue; Dave has made sure that is not an issue. After trying his hand at a couple other types of restaurants, this grill master found his calling with his signature barbecue sauces on heaping mounds of tender pulled pork, brisket, and ribs, all smoked in-house. Looking for a meal to serve the whole family? Try the Big Kahuna Belly Buster. Looking for a true Southern-style meal? Try the Southern catfish. If going for smokin' platters, be sure to add one of Dave's delectable signature sauces. A rotating selection of beers are always on tap.

820 Moraine Ave., 970-577-7427
smokindavesbbq.com

LICK AN ICE CREAM CONE
WHILE STROLLING DOWN
THE RIVERWALK

Nothing beats a sweet, cold ice cream cone on a hot summer day. Estes Park has several ice cream parlors but one in particular will have your taste buds watering as you walk through the door and catch a whiff of the sweet aroma. The Munchin' House creates all-natural, locally handcrafted ice cream in 40 different flavors. If ice cream isn't your cup of tea, try some of their homemade fudge, caramel corn, or other sweet treats. After narrowing down your flavor choice, grab a couple of napkins and then head out to the Riverwalk just outside their back door. This paved, one-mile, shaded section of trail along the banks of the Big Thompson and Fall Rivers offers a tranquil stroll through downtown Estes Park as it winds through plazas and past stores, coffee shops, restaurants, and galleries. The trail also connects with the free parking garage behind the Estes Park Visitor Center.

130 E Elkhorn Ave., 970-586-8483
themunchinhouse.com

DELIGHT IN A GOURMET MEAL
AT TWIN OWLS STEAKHOUSE

Not all trips to Estes Park are about hiking, fishing, or boating. Estes Park is also an ideal location for a destination wedding, special anniversary, family reunion, birthday dinner, or just a weekend away to celebrate your love for each other. For these occasions, have dinner at Twin Owls Steakhouse, the premiere fine dining experience in Estes Park. Located at Taharaa Mountain Lodge, Twin Owls Steakhouse offers an extensive selection of steaks, wild game, seafood, and seasonal specialties. In particular, the bone-in bison ribeye melts in your mouth. Top that with two jumbo sea scallops, a rarity to find in Estes Park, for a decadent dining experience. The restaurant is open daily at 5 p.m. unless there is a private event; reservations are highly recommended.

3110 S St. Vrain Ave., 970-586-9344
taharaa.com/twin-owls-steakhouse

PAIR EXCELLENT BEER WITH LOCAL SOUND
AT THE ROCK INN MOUNTAIN TAVERN

In the early days of Rocky Mountain National Park, the entrance used to be south of the Rock Inn Mountain Tavern. Today, two entrances welcome visitors farther north but the Rock Inn continues to maintain the original feel of rustic Estes Park, including two wood-burning stoves that warm the dining room during the winter and a large, mounted bull moose above the stage. The original log cabin–style building housed a sandwich shop in 1937. A dance hall, which is now used as the stage and dining room, was added on in 1943 to accommodate the Big Band Era. Today's chef-inspired menu of hand-crafted, hearty, comfort food and wide selection of beers make this a local favorite for winding down after a busy day at work. The scrumptious bison meatballs, in particular, will fill your belly and energize your body for another day on the trail. Different musicians perform onstage just about every evening. The Inn is open daily at 4 p.m. Reservations are not accepted, but call-ahead seating is available.

1675 State Hwy. 66, 970-586-4116
rockinnestes.com

SAVOR THE BIGGEST CINNAMON ROLLS IN TOWN
BEFORE THEY ARE GONE

The hours on the sign outside remind you every time you drive by: Open every day from 7:30 to 10 a.m. It should also say, "or until sold out," as they often do sell out of their delicious baked indulgences long before 10 a.m. Cinnamon's Bakery makes the largest cinnamon rolls in town, but it isn't just their size that makes this sweet breakfast treat so popular. The warm, soft dough topped with cream cheese frosting definitely is not on any dieter's menu. Cinnamon's keeps their menu simple with just five roll options: classic (with as much or as little frosting as you like), sticky pecan rolls, raisin-filled, salted caramel, and a daily changing fruit roll. Don't want to risk missing out? Order a day ahead to guarantee your order.

920 W Elkhorn Ave., 970-480-1501
cinnamonsestespark.com

FIND YOUR FAVORITE PIE
AT THE BEST DESSERT PLACE IN TOWN

Voted the best place for dessert in the *Estes Park Trail-Gazette* 2022 Reader's Choice Awards, You Need Pie offers a daily rotating menu of 20 to 30 pies out of a total 80 different pie varieties. In addition to the traditional favorites, like apple, cherry, and blueberry, their menu also includes unique favorites like blackberry mango, cherry rhubarb, raspberry peach, bourbon pecan, and so many others. All custom-order pies are available with crumb topping, pastry topping, or a lattice pastry top. Add a scoop of ice cream for an á-la-mode treat. You Need Pie also offers a full diner-style breakfast, lunch, and dinner menu with diner favorites like meatloaf, hand-dipped chicken tenders, Reuben sandwiches, or—a local favorite—the Monte Cristo. Found a pie you love? Order throughout the year and ship it home.

509 Big Thompson Ave., Ste. 300, 970-577-PIES (7437)
youneedpie.com

HAVE A DATE NIGHT
AT BIRD AND JIM

One of Estes Park's newest favorites, Bird and Jim is a modern mountain dining experience with a local ingredient–driven kitchen and a seasonal menu. With ingredients sourced from local farms and ranches in Estes Park, Drake, Hygiene, and other Colorado towns, along with an atmosphere that mixes casual dining with fine features, Bird and Jim is the ideal location for a date night or special event with friends. In addition to a tasty menu—including the savory buffalo burger—Bird and Jim's sommelier personally selects wine for the restaurant's extensive wine list. This is just one reason they have been featured in numerous articles and have won several *Wine Spectator* awards. Fun bit of trivia: Bird and Jim is named after two Estes Park historical pioneers, Isabella Bird, one of the first women to summit Longs Peak, and Mountain Jim, a ruffian mountain guide befriended by Bird.

915 Moraine Ave., 970-586-9832
birdandjim.com

JUMP START YOUR DAY WITH COFFEE AND ELK BUGLING
AT KIND COFFEE

Another *Trail-Gazette* Reader's Choice favorite, Kind Coffee is popular with locals for their strong mission of being good to the environment, their commitment to giving back, and their creation of a laid-back atmosphere. Kind Coffee is also one of the best spots in downtown to buy a cup of coffee, tea, or shake and then head out to their patio along the Riverwalk to watch elk during the fall rut or people any other time of year. Don't have time for sitting on the patio? Pick up a one-pound bag of their certified organic, fresh-roasted, shade-grown coffees to brew at home or order online to ship any time of year. This meeting place—they have a large, comfortable room for friendly gatherings or business meetings—attracts coffee connoisseurs and novices alike. They also offer a full food menu for breakfast or lunch. Kind Coffee opens daily at 6:30 a.m.

470 E Elkhorn Ave., 970-586-5206
kindcoffee.com

TRY A BREAKFAST PLATTER
AT THE LOCALS' FAVORITE BREAKFAST RESTAURANT

Since 1972, the Big Horn Restaurant has been serving breakfast, lunch, and dinner at their cozy, mountain-themed location on the west end of downtown Estes Park. The Big Horn offers a full menu with a wide variety of hearty platters, like Southern-style fried chicken, Rocky Mountain rainbow trout, and elk burgers, but it is their breakfast menu that steals the show. Often ranked as one of the best breakfast restaurants in town over the years, the Big Horn serves up button-popping meals sure to get you energized for the trail, or maybe to slow down and enjoy the mountain views. Menu items, which are served daily from 6 a.m. to 2 p.m., include croissant sandwiches, corned beef hash, country-fried steak, and the tasty blueberry fluffy pancakes.

401 W Elkhorn Ave., 970-586-2792
estesparkbighorn.com

TAKE IN THE AWE-INSPIRING VIEW OF LONGS PEAK
AT THE GOLF COURSE
CLUBHOUSE RESTAURANT

Longs Peak, at 14,259 feet, holds the title of the tallest mountain in Rocky Mountain National Park. Visible from as far away as Denver on a clear day, the square-top mountain juts out of the skyline from most places in Estes Park. One of the best spots to enjoy its view, however, is from the deck of the Hangar at the Estes Park 18-Hole Golf Course. On a hot summer day, this deck commands the best spot in town for a beer, a view, and a relaxing time with friends. If you would like to have a meal, the clubhouse is also home to Mother's Cafe, serving breakfast and lunch from April to October. If you prefer cooler days, come out to the Hangar in September and October to watch from the safety of the deck as bull elk chase the cows around the golf course during their annual mating season.

1480 Golf Course Rd., 970-586-8146
evrpd.com

INDULGE IN A PIZZA
FROM A WORLD CHAMPION PIZZA MAKER

Every mountain town in Colorado has at least one pizza shop. Estes Park not only has a pizza shop, but it also has one whose owner is a world champion pizza maker. The World Pizza Champions Team recently asked Antonio "Anthony" DeSousa of Antonio's Pizza to join their team of elite pizza professionals, an honor bestowed upon only the best in the industry based on skill, character, selfless effort, and an industry-wide standard of excellence. Anthony, a native of Long Island, is very particular about his ingredients, and it shows in some of the best-tasting, authentic, New York–style pizza in Colorado. If you want to enjoy leftovers, go for the New York–style 26" pizza called the Mega Don (also a great option for a large group). Beyond pizza, Antonio's also offers an oversized calzone and some excellent pasta dishes, as well as a selection of New York–style desserts like cheesecake and cannoli, but it is the pizza that makes this one of the busiest restaurants in town. You will forget about every minute you waited after the first bite.

1560 Big Thompson Ave., 970-586-7275
antonios.pizza

SPOIL YOUR TASTE BUDS
WITH THE BEST MARGARITA IN TOWN

Estes Park is said to have produced a good number of competitive rock climbers. Several were born and raised here, including Tommy Caldwell, star of the movie *The Dawn Wall*. Walking into Ed's Cantina and Grill in downtown Estes Park reminds you of how this town has become one of the best climbing locations in the US. The walls are filled with autographed photos and memorabilia from the various climbers who have passed through the door at this popular Mexican restaurant. But the signatures on the walls are not the reason for this location's popularity; it is their lively atmosphere and the best margaritas in town, including a margarita flight of three different flavors: house, spicy, and strawberry. A staple of Estes Park since 1989, Ed's Cantina and Grill also offers an authentic menu of central Mexican cuisine with a Colorado twist.

390 E Elkhorn Ave., 970-586-2919
edscantina.com

MAKE THE GHOSTS JEALOUS BY ENJOYING A WHISKEY FLIGHT
AT THE STANLEY HOTEL

Walk back into an age of decadence, when details mattered in architecture and showing your wealth communicated your arrival into society. That was the goal of F. O. Stanley when he built his hotel below Lumpy Ridge in Estes Park. The beauty of a room can also transport you back in time, and that is the feeling you get when sitting at the Whiskey Bar and Lounge at Cascades Restaurant in the Stanley Hotel. Boasting Colorado's largest selection of whiskeys and single malt scotches, this dark but ornate room in a Georgian Colonial Revival architectural style will transport you to the Roaring Twenties as you sip on a glass of this distinctive drink from one of the more than 1,200 bottles of whiskeys in the hotel's collection. If whiskey is not your style, try a Redrum Punch, a name taken right out of Stephen King's *The Shining*, a story inspired by the Stanley Hotel.

333 Wonderview Ave., 970-577-4000
stanleyhotel.com

REWARD YOURSELF WITH A DONUT HAUS DOZEN
ON THE WAY TO YOUR HIKE

The seasonally open Trail Ridge Store is the only place in the park that sells food, so picking up treats before entering Rocky Mountain National Park will keep your tummy from growling and the kids from getting cranky. And what kid wouldn't say "yes" to a glazed donut? The Donut Haus has been an Estes Park tradition since 1975 when a Phillips 66 gas station was converted into a bakery at the corner of Crags Drive and Moraine Avenue. In 2020, the original building was demolished and the owners of the Donut Haus found yet another gas station from which to sell their popular baked treat—the Tiny Town Eagle Stop Sinclair gas station. The same recipes are used today as when the original shop opened in 1975, and include favorites like sticky buns, turtles, twists, sugared raspberry-filled, and chocolate-topped buttermilk cake donuts. Be sure to go early; donuts frequently sell out by mid-morning.

860 Moraine Ave., 970-586-2988
donuthaus-estespark.com

WANT SOME NOSTALGIA WITH THAT SWEET TREAT?
GO TO ROCKET FIZZ

Estes Park is proud to be a family-friendly town and that means having lots for the kids to do, including eating treats to satisfy their cravings for delicious desserts. The best place in town to find a unique selection of sweet treats is Rocket Fizz. Parents will enjoy wandering the aisles as well, since many of the candies are vintage flavors from the good old days. Shoppers will find unique soda flavors like bacon, coffee, and swamp juice; a wide selection of candies not available anywhere else; metal lunchboxes popular with kids in the 1950s, '60s, and '70s with traditional and current licensed characters; and a wall full of saltwater taffy treats.

356 E Elkhorn Ave., Ste. 3, 970-577-1688
rocketfizz.com

MUSIC
AND ENTERTAINMENT

SEE DEEP INTO SPACE
AT THE ESTES PARK
MEMORIAL OBSERVATORY

Every year there are unique celestial events—from unexpected comets to meteor showers to planets aligning in the sky to lunar eclipses. The high elevation of Estes Park at about a mile and a half above sea level means the skies are a little bit clearer, giving stargazers unique opportunities to see deep into space. This fact, and a dedication to fostering a love of astronomy in memory of two family members gone too soon from this Earthly world, led the Connolly family to establish the Estes Park Memorial Observatory. Built in 2009, the observatory created a fun way to use astronomy to build an interest in science and math for elementary, middle, and high school kids. Equipment includes a top-of-the-line, Paramount ME II, robotic mount installed in 2014 and a 16-inch Ritchey-Chretien telescope, both synchronized through software to allow rapid and precise pointing to celestial objects. A group of volunteers maintains the equipment and offers free tours of the night sky from the observatory's 16-foot dome. Tours are available Friday through Monday nights, except two nights before and the night of the full moon in spring, summer, and fall.

1500 Manford Ave., 970-586-5668
angelsabove.org

DANCE A JIG
AT THE LONGS PEAK SCOTTISH-IRISH HIGHLAND FESTIVAL

Have a little Scottish blood in you? Have you ever met other members of your clan? Then the Longs Peak Scottish-Irish Highland Festival might be just the unique experience you need to rekindle your Celtic heritage. Over the years, more than 100 clans have participated in the festival. It also seems like every year Mother Nature decides she likes attending the Longs Peak Scottish-Irish Highland Festival in Estes Park by bringing clouds and cool, damp weather—reminiscent of Scottish and Irish coastal weather—at least one day during this three-day event. That makes this extravaganza—one of the largest of its kind in the US—that much more authentic. During this annual September festival, men throughout Estes Park sport their finest kilts and other Scottish wardrobe accessories. Participants at the festival can listen to Celtic music, compete in dog and highland cattle competitions, watch the strongman Scottish challenge, enjoy whiskey tastings for beginners or master enthusiasts, and much more. Started in 1976, this festival brings together participants, visitors, and locals to celebrate Celtic tradition, including a parade—complete with bagpipers and more kilts—through downtown Estes Park on the Saturday of the festival.

scotfest.com

LEAF PEEP
ALONG THE PEAK-TO-PEAK SCENIC BYWAY

Each fall, thousands of people flock to Colorado to enjoy the fall colors. One of the most spectacular displays of autumn foliage in northern Colorado is the Peak-to-Peak Scenic Byway, which stretches 55 miles from Estes Park to US Interstate 70 near Idaho Springs. This lovely drive, all on paved roadway, was established in 1918 as the first scenic byway in Colorado. This stretch of road makes a great day trip from Estes Park, passing views of Longs Peak and Mount Meeker, the St. Malo's Chapel, views of the Continental Divide, the quaint town of Nederland, a few abandoned mines, the gambling town of Black Hawk, and out to the former mining town of Idaho Springs. With minimal stopping, the drive takes about three hours but with leaf peeping, plan on a full-day tour. Towns with restaurants are few but Nederland has some options for sandwiches, ice cream, or pizza, and the casinos in Black Hawk have a wide selection of eateries. Keep your eye out for moose sightings along the drive. Timing for the best leaf color can be tough to predict because many factors can affect the vibrancy and timing of the brightest yellows and golds but typically, the colors peak during the last two weeks of September.

Directions and photo spots: Start on Colorado Highway 7 in Estes Park and drive south. Continue south for 18 miles and make a right onto Colorado Highway 72. Travel 22 miles south on Colorado Highway 72 towards the town of Nederland. At the roundabout in Nederland, take the first exit to the right following Colorado Highway 119 for 19 miles towards Black Hawk. Continue on Colorado Highway 119 through Black Hawk and then make a right at the traffic light for US Highway 6 towards Interstate 70. US Highway 6 will merge with US Interstate 70 in seven miles from the traffic light.

THINGS TO SEE ALONG THE WAY

Lily Lake in Rocky Mountain National Park for fall color photos
Saint Catherine of Siena, Chapel on the Rock at St. Malo Retreat Center
Brainard Lake Recreation Area
Golden Gate Canyon State Park
Rollins Pass out of Rollinsville
Black Hawk

• •

KICK UP YOUR BOOTS
AT ROOFTOP RODEO, THE LONGEST RUNNING, HIGH-ELEVATION RODEO IN THE US

There are rodeos, and then there is Estes Park's rodeo. Rooftop Rodeo, the longest running, high-elevation rodeo in the US at 7,522 feet, takes viewers back to small, old-time Western competitions even though it is a high-profile, Professional Rodeo Cowboys Association (PRCA)–sanctioned event. Held in early July every year since 1908 (except during World War II and COVID-19), this award-winning community event brings some of the biggest names in professional rodeo to the Rocky Mountains from around the world, including past world champions. But you don't have to be a cowboy or cowgirl to appreciate this week-long celebration. Events include bull riding, steer wrestling, bareback riding, saddle bronc riding, tie-down roping, team roping, and more. Do not miss the adrenaline-pumping cowgirls as they speed through a barrel racing course. Mutton bustin' and cash catch are always popular events for the kids, and no rodeo would be complete without a Rodeo Queen and her attendant. So, break out your cowboy hat and boots and head over to the Granny May Arena at Estes Park Fairgrounds. In addition to the rodeo, there is a parade of draft horses, antique cars, cowboys, bands, and more to kick off the week of festivities.

1209 Manford Ave., 970-586-6104
rooftoprodeo.com

● ●

RACE YOUR DUCK
IN THE ESTES PARK DUCK RACE

These ducks don't quack but they sure do cause a ruckus. The Estes Park Duck Race, held the first Saturday in May every year, sees thousands of yellow rubber duckies drop from the starting line at Nicky's Resort and then float down Fall River. All the ducks' sponsors cheer them on from the banks of the river, each hoping his/her duck crosses the finish line at George Hix Memorial Riverside Plaza before the other competitors for a chance to win $15,000 in cash or hundreds of other prizes. The event, which includes a festival with live music, beer garden, and 5K waddle, is a blast for visitors and locals of all ages, but it also raises funds for more than 60 Estes Valley charities. Each duck is "adopted" for a fee and the sponsor selects the non-profit to receive the proceeds of their adoption. Since the race started in 1989, nearly $3 million have been raised for organizations providing non-profit or charitable services in Estes Valley. As part of the fun activities, you can take a selfie with race mascot, Lucky Duck, and see more duck "stuff" than in any other place in Colorado.

Nicky's Resort
1360 Fall River Rd., 970-586-5377
epduckrace.org

TAKE A FAMILY PHOTO
AT THE ESTES PARK WELCOME SIGN

No visit to Estes Park would be complete without a family, group, or selfie photo at the Estes Park stone welcome sign. Although there are several great locations for photos to document a trip to this mountain town, the sign at the mouth of the St. Vrain Canyon just before dropping down into the valley commands the best view of this stunning region. But don't just stop, snap a photo, and then travel into town. Relax for a few minutes to enjoy the first view the original settlers saw as they made the difficult journey up the canyon on dirt trails. Imagine this valley, surrounded by the peaks of the Continental Divide, free of homes, hotels, shops, and roads, and full of elk, deer, and other big game. At that time, the Big Thompson River meandered through the meadow below where Lake Estes now fills the basin since the flow of the river was stopped by the Olympus Dam in 1948. This location provides a pretty location for watching a sunrise or sunset, and a few eager beggars—golden-mantled ground squirrels, chipmunks, black-billed magpies, and Stellar's jays—will scurry around the parking lot for your amusement.

The sign is located along US Highway 36
about a half mile before Mall Road.

PHOTO HOTSPOTS FOR A FAMILY MEMORY

Mountain lion statue in George Hix Riverside Plaza

Enos Mills statue on the northeast corner of Bond Park

Bridge over Big Thompson River at Lake Estes

Birch Ruins and trails at Centennial Open Space
at Knoll-Willows

Front porch of the Stanley Hotel

Top of the parking garage

VIEW THE TOWN AND MOUNTAINS FROM ABOVE
ON THE ESTES PARK AERIAL TRAMWAY

Opened to the public in July 1955, the Estes Park Aerial Tramway represents a unique, free-span design where the wire ropes are only connected to the towers at the bottom and top stations. This type of tramway, more common in Europe than in the US, works well on steep terrain like that of Prospect Mountain where the tramway operates. But beyond the unique design, this tramway also has one of the most unique perspectives of Estes Park, taking riders up nearly 1,400 feet in five minutes to a birds-eye view of Estes Valley and the surrounding mountain peaks. Once at the top, visitors can take in the sweeping vista of Longs Peak to the south, Lumpy Ridge to the north, and the Continental Divide to the west. A coffee shop, gift shop, and several picnic areas are located at the top along with a few short trails to take in the views from different directions. Tickets are sold on a first-come, first-served basis. The Estes Park Aerial Tramway is open daily from 9 a.m. to 6 p.m. Memorial Day Weekend to Labor Day Weekend. They are open 9 a.m. to 6 p.m. on Saturdays and Sundays only in September (after Labor Day).

420 E Riverside Dr., 970-475-4094
estestram.com

IMPRESS YOUR FAMILY
WITH YOUR PUTT-PUTT SKILLS

What summer vacation wouldn't be complete without a round of putt-putt golf? Estes Park strives to maintain its family destination feel—and the local teens need places for dates, too—so several miniature golf courses are available throughout town. These courses are further enhanced by the surrounding splendor of Estes Park. The courses range in price, skill level, histories, and creative hole features like alligators, waterfalls, mines, and caves.

Cascade Creek Mini Golf (offers two courses)
Mountain Course and Meadows Course, located at Ride-A-Kart
2250 Big Thompson Ave., 970-586-6495
rideakart.com

Meadow Mini Golf located at Trout Haven Resorts
840 Moraine Ave., 970-577-0202
trouthavenresorts.com/miniature-golf

Fun City (offers two courses)
455 Prospect Village Dr., 970-586-2828
funcityofestes.com

RIDE
THE RAINBOW SLIDE

You have heard the commercial voiceover talent say, "Ride the rainbow." Well, you actually can in Estes Park. Although there isn't a pot of gold at the end of it, the giant rainbow slide is sure to put smiles on the faces of children of all ages. Located at Fun City of Estes Park, this sack slide on steroids can't be missed as you drive from downtown Estes Park towards the southern entrance to Rocky Mountain National Park. In business since 1969, this popular family fun park will get the kids tuckered out and generate lots of fun memories for the whole family. Fun City also offers go-karts, a bungee trampoline, bumper cars, bumper boats, gemstone panning, and water-walking balls. Take advantage of Fun City's value cards, which can be purchased at Fun City's entrance, for the best pricing. Hours vary by season, but they are closed in winter.

455 Prospect Village Dr., 970-586-2828
funcityofestes.com

EXPERIENCE THE THRILLS
OF A MOUNTAIN ROLLERCOASTER

The newest alpine coaster in Colorado and the closest one to
Denver, Boulder, and Fort Collins, this unique family experience
will have you screaming through the ponderosa forest on the
east side of Estes Park. With views of Longs Peak, Mustang
Mountain Coaster gives riders a chance to speed through the
trees at their own pace—screaming fast around the curves or
a gentle coast across the mountainside of Sombrero Ranch.
Mountain, or alpine, coasters first appeared in the Alps of
Austria in 1996 to mimic a bobsled ride. Switching from the
trough of a bobsled coaster to tracks allows the mountain coaster
to be unhindered by snow or ice and therefore stay open all year
long. Riders on Mustang Mountain Coaster control their speed
using a lever brake system throughout the 2,043-foot-long ride
that takes about four minutes. Open year-round, but the hours
vary by season.

1180 Dry Gulch Rd., 970-672-1829
mustangmountaincoaster.com

COMPLETE
THE "PIKAS IN THE PARK" SCAVENGER HUNT

Pikas are small mammals of the rabbit family that live their entire lives above the tree line. Found throughout the tundra and in some lower elevations of Rocky Mountain National Park, they do not hibernate but rather collect plants all summer to feed on throughout the cold winter months in Colorado's mountains. This rugged yet charismatic animal is a perfect symbol for the uniqueness of Estes Park. For the centennial celebration in 2017, the Town of Estes Park developed the Pikas in the Park Scavenger Hunt, an interactive family activity that incorporates some history about Estes Park and a tour of downtown using life-sized bronze sculptures of these animals. There are 12 pikas placed throughout downtown Estes Park and an activity guide will help pika seekers on their hunt. Once all 12 are located, head over to the Estes Park Visitor Center to claim your Pika Finder button.

Estes Park Visitor Center
500 Big Thompson Ave., 970-577-9900
visitestespark.com/things-to-do/kids-and-family-activities/pikas-in-the-park

WATCH
THE "CATCH THE GLOW" PARADE

Kids of all ages love to watch a holiday parade and wait for Santa Claus to make an appearance at the end of the line of floats, bands, and characters. Not many parades, however, happen at night with floats decked out in every color of LED light imaginable. Held on the Friday night after Thanksgiving, this dazzling annual tradition brings out locals and visitors from all over the Front Range. As many as 20,000 people line Elkhorn Avenue to watch this whimsical holiday procession. With more than 40 floats and other decked-out vehicles, this cheery holiday event will be sure to get you into the spirit of Christmas. The parade starts at 5:30 p.m. Visitors are encouraged to use the free parking garage. A free trolley service is also available before, during, and after the parade.

Parade start
400 block of W Elkhorn Ave. (West Park Center)

Parade end
Intersection of US Highway 34 and US Highway 36 (near McDonald's)

estesparkeventscomplex.com/catch-the-glow-parade

DRESS UP IN COSTUME
FOR THE DOWNTOWN
HALLOWEEN FESTIVAL

In a town where elk, deer, black bears, and the occasional moose wander around the streets at night; neighborhoods are dark; sidewalks are rare; and homes are spread apart, encouraging kids to go out to trick-or-treat doesn't seem like a wise idea. Instead, the Town of Estes Park decided to manage trick-or-treating Estes Park style. Since 1983, downtown Estes Park is closed off to traffic along Elkhorn Avenue to allow families to participate in trick-or-treating the mountain way. More than 60 businesses stay open to hand out candies, caramel-covered apples, and other treats for locals and visiting kids who come up for the unique celebration on Halloween night. Adults and children alike adorn costumes of all shapes and sizes, a haunted ambulance is ready to help, and dancers recreate Michael Jackson's "Thriller" zombie moves in the main intersection. Admission is free for this event, which is held annually on Halloween night from 5 p.m. to 8 p.m.

OTHER HALLOWEEN FESTIVITIES IN ESTES PARK

The Shining Ball at the Stanley Hotel
(sells out fast; black tie event)

Pumpkins and Pilsners at Bond Park
in downtown Estes Park

Halloween Spooktacular at YMCA of the Rockies

Family Fall Festival at Trout Haven Resorts

Kid-friendly Haunted House at the American Legion

BE ASTOUNDED
BY ONE OF COLORADO'S LONGEST
FOURTH OF JULY FIREWORKS SHOWS

Not many Colorado towns are home to one of the best script writers and designers of a fireworks show in the industry. Estes Park is lucky that way, and it shows in the 25-minute display showcasing the almost 2,000 fireworks that light up the sky above Lake Estes. The Town of Estes Park estimates more than 20,000 people attend the show on the evening of the Fourth of July, with license plates revealing travelers from all over the US in attendance. The artistry of the show includes a variety of unique fireworks, like horsetails, willows, jellyfish, hearts, USA in letters, plus ground displays. The show starts at approximately 9 p.m. and is launched from Fisherman's Nook at Lake Estes.

BEST SPOTS TO WATCH THE ESTES PARK FOURTH OF JULY FIREWORKS SHOW

Centennial Open Space at Knoll-Willows (photo hotspot)

Lake Estes 9-Hole Golf Course

Cherokee Draw on the south side of Lake Estes

Gem Lake Trail in Rocky Mountain National Park
(photo hotspot)

Estes Valley Community Center parking lot

Deck at the Bull Pin bowling lanes

Top of the Estes Park parking garage

Kruger Rock Trail in Hermit Park Open Space
(photo hotspot)

Top of Pole Hill Road (photo hotspot)

SLIDE THROUGH THE TUBE INTO THE POOL
AT THE ESTES VALLEY COMMUNITY CENTER

For those who seek out thrills, check out this spiraling tube water slide that drops into the deep portion of the recreational pool at the Estes Valley Community Center. If the tube slide is not for you, the aquatic center also keeps visitors entertained with a lazy river, a lap pool with a climbing wall, an outdoor hot tub, and animal-themed water features (the only place in town where you can have a bear dump a bucket of water on you or have a fish or moose douse you with spray). This is a great way for the family to cool down on a hot summer afternoon. The community center is also a full-service recreation center with indoor basketball courts (sometimes set up for indoor tennis and pickle ball), weights, dance rooms, an indoor golf simulator, and an indoor walking track. The Center is open daily, but the hours vary by season.

660 Community Dr., 970-586-8191
evrpd.com

PLAY A GAME OF DISC GOLF
AT ONE OF TWO COURSES IN ESTES PARK

Disc golf has grown in popularity in the last few years, and what better way to get an introduction to this fun sport than in a place with amazing mountain scenery. There are two courses in Estes Park: one at the Lake Estes 9-Hole Golf Course and the other on the YMCA of the Rockies campus. The Lake Estes 9-Hole Golf Course opens daily at 12 p.m. throughout the year and the public is welcome. Watch out for elk on the course during the spring calving season and fall mating season. The YMCA of the Rockies course is spread throughout their campus and requires an approximately four-mile walk to complete the 18-hole course. It is available to guests, members, and day-pass holders.

Lake Estes 9-Hole Golf Course
690 Big Thompson Ave., 970-586-8176
evrpd.com

YMCA of the Rockies
199 Program Way, 970-586-3341, ext. 1104
ymcarockies.org

DRESS UP IN
WILD WEST COSTUMES
FOR A FAMILY PORTRAIT

A visit to Estes Park does not have to be rugged, rustic, or remote; many modern comforts exist in this small mountain town. Although the area has kept up with the times over the decades, parts of it still feel like the Old West. Log cabins dot the landscape of the nearby mountain valleys, elk continue to roam through the forests, and dirt roads still take curious explorers deep into the backcountry away from modernization. There is no reason, therefore, why a visit can't include a temporary walk back in time for a fun, old-time portrait of you, your family members, and/or your friends. Estes Park has two portrait shops, each with its own style of photography and collection of costumes and props. Hours vary for both shops based on the season.

Memories Old Time Portraits
132 W Elkhorn Ave., 970-586-5568
memoriesoldtimeportraits.com

Real West Old Time Portraits
103 W Elkhorn Ave., 970-586-9378
facebook.com/realwestportraits

CELEBRATE "ELKTOBER"
AT ELK FEST

Estes Park has its own herd of elk, which the human residents thoroughly enjoy. Approximately 600 to 800 elk live in Estes Valley, moving between the foothills and the tundra, depending on the time of year. During the fall, elk go through their mating season. Called a "rut," this annual display of ruminant reproduction not only attracts the bulls and cows to each other but also brings visitors to Estes Valley to watch the action. This is when the town of Estes Park hosts their annual Elk Fest weekend in downtown Bond Park. Held the first full weekend in October, Elk Fest is a free, family-friendly festival with vendors, live music, food trucks, bugling contests, Native American cultural presentations, live raptors, wildlife education, performances, and much more to celebrate all things elk. Remember that elk, even in downtown Estes Park, are wild and unpredictable. Keep a safe distance and be respectful of their space.

Bond Park
170 MacGregor Ave.
estesparkeventscomplex.com/elk-fest

49

WIND DOWN
WITH FREE OUTDOOR CONCERTS
THROUGHOUT THE SUMMER

Estes Park stays busy all summer with regular weekend festivals and events downtown, many hiking trails, and a plethora of stores for shopping along Elkhorn Avenue. Consequently, it is no surprise that the town of Estes Park also provides free summer concerts to help locals and visitors wind down after a busy day. Locations for concerts include Bond Park, Performance Park, Lake Estes Marina, Coffee on the Rocks, and the Inn on Fall River. Estes Park also hosts a few summer music festivals, including the Friends of Folk Music Festival, the Big Bang! Concert on Fourth of July, and the SnowyGrass Music Festival. The lineup changes each summer but schedules can be found on Visit Estes Park's website.

Bond Park
170 MacGregor Ave.

Performance Park
435 W Elkhorn Ave.

Lake Estes Marina
1770 Big Thompson Ave., 970-586-2011

Coffee on the Rocks
510 Moraine Ave., 719-250-4829

Inn on Fall River
1660 Fall River Rd., 800-255-4118

visitestespark.com

WATCH A MOVIE
AT THE OLDEST SINGLE-SCREEN MOVIE THEATER IN THE US

Movie theaters have taken on a whole new level of presentation in recent years, with stadium seating, high-performance digital sound systems, and reclining leather seats. There is something to be said, however, for the authentic feel of an old-fashioned movie theater built at a time when Charlie Chaplin commanded the top spot on the marquee. Completed in 1915, the Historic Park Theatre is the oldest continuously operating single-screen movie theater in the US. The 224-seat theater, which is on the National Register of Historic Places, still has the feel of an early cinema house, with dark red velvet curtains, tapestries on the walls, and wooden seats. Recent owners, however, recognized the need to modernize movie screenings and updated the theater with a new screen, new digital projector with a Dolby 3D system, and new Dolby 5.1 surround sound system. Check their listings for returning screenings of favorite movies from past decades, such as *Poltergeist*, *One Week* (starring Buster Keaton), *Dr. No*, and *Star Trek: The Wrath of Khan*. The theater also hosts live events and is open year-round.

130 Moraine Ave., 970-586-8904
historicparktheatre.com

GROOVE WITH ONE OF ESTES PARK'S
MOST INTERESTING PEOPLE— COWBOY BRAD FITCH

If you walk down a street in Estes Park and think you have seen the ghost of John Denver, you have actually seen the next best thing. Cowboy Brad Fitch has an uncanny resemblance to this popular folk singer who died in a plane crash in 1997, but Fitch has his own style and a tremendous following in Colorado. Specializing in original folk music, classic cowboy tunes, and, yes, the songs of John Denver, Fitch, who was born and raised in Estes Park, has been playing music professionally since he was 15 years old. Playing more than 300 concerts a year and having 23 albums to his name, this singer, songwriter, and guitar player gets the crowd to their feet with his contagious smile and fun songs. Check his website for the latest concert and performance dates.

cowboybrad.com

Kayak Lake Estes

SPORTS
AND RECREATION

HIKE TO THE THUMB
IN THE THUMB OPEN SPACE

The region around Estes Park is full of rock outcroppings and mountain peaks with unique names chosen to describe the shape of the feature: Notchtop, Twin Owls, Flattop, Knobtop, and Lumpy Ridge, to name a few. The one closest to town is the Thumb. Located on the southeastern side of Prospect Mountain, this 8,400-foot crag juts out from the rest of the mountain, giving the appearance of a thumbs-up sign. The Thumb Open Space is the newest recreation area purchased by the Town of Estes Park. Acquired on May 26, 2021, and opened to the public on July 1, 2022, this 65-acre park transitioned from a popular but private hiking and climbing destination to a public open space with high-quality bouldering and nearly 50 rock-climbing routes of all levels. It also has one trail on the property: a 0.85-mile platted trail that gains 500 feet in elevation as it rises to the top of Prospect Mountain with additional access routes to the Thumb and Needles rock outcroppings. The Thumb Open Space Trailhead and parking lot is located on Peak View Drive one mile west of Colorado Highway 7. The area is open daily from sunrise to sunset.

estespark.colorado.gov/thumb

START YOUR DAY WITH A SUNRISE
AT SPRAGUE LAKE

There are unlimited numbers of scenic locations in Rocky Mountain National Park that are ideal for watching the start of a new day, but one of the most iconic is Sprague Lake. Located along Bear Lake Road, this manmade alpine lake offers views of the sun rising in the eastern sky spreading purple tones of morning light as it hits the peaks of the Rocky Mountains to the west. Keep an eye out for moose, elk, beavers, black bears, and various duck species near this lake surrounded by beaver ponds, forest, and marshes. There is a flat, 0.8-mile loop trail around the lake with several benches along the way to take in the scenery. This shallow lake is also popular for fishing. The area includes a large picnic area, trails that follow along Glacier Creek, and one of the few flush toilets in the park (open seasonally in summer). A timed-entry reservation is required to access this area of the park from 5 a.m. to 6 p.m. between Memorial Day Weekend and the second Monday in October. No reservation is needed outside of this time frame.

nps.gov/romo

MAKE THE JUMP
AT OPEN AIR ADVENTURE PARK

If Rocky Mountain National Park is crowded or timed-entry reservations are sold out, consider exploring the possibilities of the Open Air Adventure Park. Located off Moraine Avenue on the southwest side of Estes Park just minutes from downtown, this aerial challenge course encourages visitors to bring out their inner gymnast with 32 unique challenges at 11 and 21 feet in the air. Activities include hanging chairs, zip lines, tightropes, swinging logs, moving platforms, and the more technical Pirates' Crossing. While you are swinging through the ropes course, be sure to enjoy the surrounding mountain views. If you prefer to have your adventures on the ground, the park also has axe throwing. Open Air Adventure Park is an ideal location for families, school groups, family reunions, and corporate team building. The Park is open seasonally and reservations are recommended.

490 Prospect Village Dr., 970-586-3066
openairadventurepark.com

TAKE A CLASS OR TOUR
WITH ROCKY MOUNTAIN CONSERVANCY

Rocky Mountain Conservancy is a non-profit organization supporting Rocky Mountain National Park. A busy association that provides funds and volunteers for the park, they work on many projects like repairing trails, raising funds for acquiring new property, helping with fire mitigation, collecting seeds for restoration projects, building exhibits in the park, and much more. To raise the necessary funds, the Conservancy hosts a wide array of classes, tours, and other programs about wildlife, history, and the natural resources of the area. Examples of their programs include photography, journaling, wildlife viewing, watercolor painting, snowshoeing, and introduction to rock climbing. In addition, there are more than 40 free classes for kids offered each summer to teach them about geocaching, wildlife, and ecology, to name a few of the available topics. Their field courses, which were on hiatus for a couple years due to the COVID-19 pandemic, returned in 2022 with a wide array of subjects, dates, and times. Courses are offered throughout the year.

P.O. Box 3100, 970-586-0108
rmconservancy.org

EXPLORE ROCKY MOUNTAIN NATIONAL PARK
ON AN OPEN-AIR JEEP TOUR

Rocky Mountain National Park covers a lot of ground—265,847 acres to be exact—and it can take some time to familiarize yourself with its features and locations. If you are only visiting for a day or two, a Jeep tour may be just what you need to see and learn as much as possible about the park. There are several tour companies available, each with its own style and flair. Green Jeep Tours is regularly ranked on travel sites and reader's choice awards as the best Jeep tour company in Estes Park. Working year-round—those blankets and side walls help mitigate a cold, breezy day in winter—Green Jeep Tours offers several different options depending on your goals, time, and price. If something a little wilder is your style, look into WildSide 4x4 Tours. Also open year-round for tours in Rocky Mountain National Park, WildSide is the only tour company that has off-road permits in all of Estes Park (summers only).

Green Jeep Tours
970-577-0034
greenjeeptour.com

WildSide 4x4 Tours
970-586-8687
wildside4x4tours.com

RENT A FOUR-WHEEL-DRIVE VEHICLE
TO EXPLORE THE LOCAL FORESTS

In addition to Rocky Mountain National Park, there are thousands of acres of forest to explore in nearby Roosevelt National Forest. If you are looking for a different type of adventure or want to feel like a kid again, consider renting a four-wheel-drive vehicle, like a Razor, ATV, or Jeep. Backbone Adventures offers a variety of off-road vehicles. All ATVs include a truck and trailer for towing, a full tank of gas, a GPS tablet, and a helmet to keep the noggin safe. Rentals are available in full- or half-day increments. You can rent single-person vehicles or ATVs that hold up to six people for a blast with the entire family. Their experienced team can suggest several options for nearby trails ranked easy to extreme.

1851 N Lake Ave., 970-235-5045
backbonecycles.com

DRIVE UP TRAIL RIDGE ROAD,
THE HIGHEST CONTINUOUSLY PAVED ROAD IN THE US

Opened in 1932, Trail Ridge Road is the highest continuously paved road in the US, running for 48 miles across Rocky Mountain National Park from Estes Park to Grand Lake. At its highest elevation of 12,183 feet, you have sweeping views of the open tundra and four mountain ranges: Gore Range, Never Summer Mountain Range, Medicine Bow Mountains, and Front Range. One of ten America's Byways in Colorado, this road traverses 11 miles above the tree line across open tundra, similar in look and feel to what you would experience in Alaska. Keep an eye out for elk, bighorn sheep, pikas, yellow-bellied marmots, coyotes, and various bird species. The road is typically open from Memorial Day Weekend to mid-October, depending on snow conditions, with an average winter closure date of October 23. Driving across Trail Ridge Road requires a park entry pass and a timed-entry reservation from Memorial Day Weekend to the second Monday in October from 9 a.m. to 3 p.m. The road can be driven without a timed-entry reservation before 9 a.m. and after 3 p.m., and is open 24 hours a day, seven days a week.

Rocky Mountain National Park: nps.gov/romo
Trail Ridge Road Status Line: 970-586-1222

● ●

SAFETY ON TRAIL RIDGE ROAD

Being above the tree line takes you to an elevation of 11,400 feet and higher. The air is thinner at this altitude and can cause rapid weather changes and negatively impact your body. Here are a few considerations for a drive across Trail Ridge Road.

- Bring plenty of water.
- Watch for signs of altitude sickness, which include headache, nausea, dizziness, vomiting, and fatigue.
- Bring layers of clothes in preparation for snow, wind, and cold temperatures.
- Wear sturdy hiking shoes.
- Keep snacks or food in your vehicle in case the only store with a small café at the Alpine Visitor Center is closed.
- Watch for lightning and do not stay above the tree line during a thunderstorm.
- There are steep drop-offs along Trail Ridge Road that can make some people nervous when driving across the tundra. Remember that the lanes are the same width as any other road. Pull off into a pullout if you are driving slower than other cars to allow them to pass.
- Trail Ridge Road does occasionally close during the summer season due to snow, ice, and emergencies. If this is the case and you need to get back to Estes Park or Grand Lake, the drive-around is about three hours.

VISIT THE ALPINE VISITOR CENTER,
THE HIGHEST VISITOR CENTER IN THE NATIONAL PARK SYSTEM

While on Trail Ridge Road, make a stop at the Alpine Visitor Center. Sitting at 11,796 feet and located just above the headwaters of Fall River, this is the highest elevation visitor center in the National Park System. Open seasonally during the summer, this building in the sky opened in 1965, and houses emergency medical services, park information, and restrooms. Interpretive rangers are also available to answer questions. Check out the displays inside to learn how the remote building is powered (there are no utility lines connected to it) and how it receives water (Hint: that snow around it helps). While here, test your hiking skills on the short (only 0.7 miles long) but steep (climbs 162 feet) Alpine Ridge Trail that will take your breath away with its views and decrease in available oxygen.

Rocky Mountain National Park: nps.gov/romo
Trail Ridge Road Status Line: 970-586-1222

HIKE UP
TRAIL RIDGE ROAD
BEFORE THE ROAD OPENS TO CARS

Trail Ridge Road spends more time closed than open during a single year. With high winds, icy roads, feet of snow across the tundra, and drifts as high as 22 feet along the road each winter, it is a challenging environment to visit outside of the summer season. Rocky Mountain National Park's road crew, however, starts clearing the road in April in preparation for opening the road to visitors on Memorial Day Weekend, weather permitting. As two crews—one from each side of the park—plow the road, sections of it become trails before it is opened to cars after the plow crews meet near the Alpine Visitor Center. This opportunity, which only lasts a couple of weeks each May, allows bikers and walkers to see the tundra covered in snow and enjoy a road free of vehicles. The skies are usually sunny and clear in May, making this a pleasant stroll from forest to above the tree line.

Rocky Mountain National Park: nps.gov/romo
Trail Ridge Road Status Line: 970-586-1222

CLIMB THE ROCK WALL
AT THE ESTES PARK MOUNTAIN SHOP

Estes Park is surrounded by some of the best rock-climbing routes in the Western US. But if you are new to the sport or would like to practice your skills when the weather turns bad, check out the indoor climbing gym at the Estes Park Mountain Shop. With more than 4,500 square feet of climbing terrain, including state-of-the-art training tools (Moon Board and M6 Treadwall) and 125 linear feet of bouldering, this activity should get you started on the right anchor. Switched out often, routes are available for all levels of climbers from beginners to experts. The wall is a great activity for birthday parties, team-building events, and other group activities. The shop is open year-round. Memberships and gear rental are also available.

2050 Big Thompson Ave., 970-586-6548
estesparkmountainshop.com

EXPLORE ESTES PARK'S
ROCK-CLIMBING OPPORTUNITIES

Estes Park has become a haven for rock climbers and boulderers and is home to some of America's most classic routes. With so much rocky terrain surrounding the valley, there are plenty of options for testing your climbing skills, including hiring a guide to take you on your first climb. Here are a few popular areas for climbing and a couple of companies that will take you out on a guided route.

Locations

Lumpy Ridge, Rocky Mountain National Park, accessed via the trailhead on Devil's Gulch Road

Jurassic Park, accessed by the Lily Lake Trail along Colorado Highway 7 south of Estes Park

Mary's Lake area, accessed via Mary's Lake Road, requires a permit from Estes Valley Recreation and Park District evrpd.com

Performance Park, accessed in downtown Estes Park

Guides
Estes Park Rock Climbing
They also have a rock-climbing wall
970-205-9298
estesparkrockclimbing.com

Colorado Mountain School
720-387-8944
coloradomountainschool.com

Kent Mountain Adventure Center
970-586-5990

CAPTURE A SUNSET
IN ROCKY MOUNTAIN NATIONAL PARK

Although much of the park faces east, the wide-open views along Trail Ridge Road afford both novice and advanced photographers stunning views for sunset photography. But Trail Ridge Road isn't the only place to capture a scenic sunset within the park. Because the park spans hundreds of square miles, it is important to pick out your sunset photo spot hours in advance and plan on arriving at least 30 minutes prior to sunset to catch the best colors. Along Trail Ridge Road, check out Rock Cut or Gore Range Overlook for sunset views with Longs Peak in the shot. Closer to Estes Park, stop at the Beaver Meadows Overlook—the large pullout between Upper Beaver Meadows Road and Deer Mountain Junction—for an expansive view of the mountains along the Continental Divide. (Hint: this one works well for sunrise, too.) For an alpine lake at sunset, stop at Lily Lake or Bear Lake, photographing south towards Longs Peak at either lake. All are accessible year-round except Rock Cut and Gore Range Overlook. Be sure to bring a tripod and remote shutter release to get the sharpest photo possible.

Rocky Mountain National Park: nps.gov/romo
Trail Ridge Road Status Line: 970-586-1222

VIEW THE NIGHT SKIES
FROM 12,000 FEET

Milky Way season runs from March to October in the northern hemisphere. Conveniently, Trail Ridge Road is open for much of that time frame. As you climb in elevation, the air becomes clearer and stars appear brighter, including the Milky Way. Several places along Trail Ridge Road are ideal for viewing the night sky, and Longs Peak sits in the southern portion of the park so the center of the Milky Way, which also rises into the southern sky, appears to curve over this 14,259-foot mountain. Although any place along Trail Ridge Road is great for celestial encounters, some of the better spots, especially for night photography, include Many Parks Curve, Rock Cut, Mushroom Rocks, Poudre Lake, and Lake Irene. There is less light pollution from the Front Range towns as you head west into the park.

Rocky Mountain National Park: nps.gov/romo
Trail Ridge Road Status Line: 970-586-1222

ENJOY A LEISURELY WALK
AROUND AN ALPINE LAKE

Rocky Mountain National Park is home to more than 150 lakes. From little lakes nestled into high-elevation bowls to man-made lakes created for fishing at lodges long gone from the park, there are plenty of lakes to choose for a stroll. Three lakes in particular, however, have excellent, easy beginner trails for those who need to acclimate to the elevation or want a quick outdoor adventure. The first lake is Lily Lake. Located on the south side of the park along Colorado Highway 7, Lily Lake was only added to the park in the 1990s thanks to funding from the Rocky Mountain Conservancy. Starting at an elevation of 8,930 feet, this trail only gains 29 feet of altitude. The next hike, Sprague Lake Loop, starts at a slightly lower elevation of 8,690 feet and gains 22 feet. The third lake is Bear Lake. At a much higher elevation of 9,475 feet, this walk takes a little more effort because of its higher start and 113 feet of elevation gain. All three are beautiful spots for watching a sunrise or sunset with short, handicapped-accessible trails, and they each can be accessed year-round. Lily and Sprague Lakes can be good spots to see moose while Bear Lake is beautiful for fall colors.

Rocky Mountain National Park: nps.gov/romo
Trail Ridge Road Status Line: 970-586-1222

GO HORSEBACK RIDING
IN THE ROCKY MOUNTAINS

The first settlers in Estes Valley arrived on horseback and today, visitors can still experience this more rugged method of navigating the mountains and valleys of the region. Three stables offer one-hour to all-day horseback rides in Estes Valley and Rocky Mountain National Park for riders of all skill levels. Schedule a tour on horseback with one of the companies to hear the clicking of horseshoes across rocks as you feel the wind through your hair. Jackson Stables at YMCA of the Rockies offers rides on the YMCA property and in Rocky Mountain National Park. National Park Gateway Stables, located outside the Fall River Entrance, also takes riders into the park, traversing the vast meadow of Horseshoe Park or into Roosevelt National Forest. Sombrero Stables, on the eastern side, has been in Estes Park since 1959 and offers shorter rides of 30 minutes to two hours on their private ranch.

National Park Gateway Stables
4600 Fall River Rd., 970-586-5269
skhorses.com

Jackson Stables
2515 Tunnel Rd., 970-586-3341
jacksonstables.com

Sombrero Stables
1895 Big Thompson Ave., 970-533-8155
sombrero.com/sombrero-stables

RENT A BIKE, PEDAL CART, KAYAK, OR BOAT
AT LAKE ESTES MARINA

Lake Estes, dedicated in 1949 after the construction of the Olympus Dam, is a centerpiece for recreation in the town of Estes Park. With a 3.75-mile paved trail around the lake, stocked waters for fishing, and astounding views of the Rocky Mountains, renting one of several modes of transportation from the Lake Estes Marina can help you enjoy this gem on a summer afternoon. Open from May through September, the marina rents bikes, pedal carts, kayaks, paddle boats, and pontoon boats for exploring the area by land or water. The marina also has a store full of supplies for a day at the lake, including snacks, drinks, fishing supplies, hats, shirts, and fishing licenses.

1770 Big Thompson Ave., 970-586-2011
evrpd.com

TIP

After stopping at the Lake Estes Marina for supplies, well-stocked Lake Estes may be the first place anglers go when trying their hand at fishing in Estes Valley, but you may want to try these other hot spots as well. The last four on this list are within Rocky Mountain National Park. The park has special fishing regulations, which can be reviewed at nps.gov/romo/planyourvisit/fishing.htm. All locations require a Colorado fishing license, which can be purchased at the Lake Estes Marina, Kirks Flyshop, Estes Angler, or Scot's Sporting Goods.

Big Thompson River below Lake Estes
Mary's Lake
Fern Lake
Glacier Creek
Sprague Lake
Fall River

PLAY A
SHORT ROUND OF GOLF
AT THE LAKE ESTES 9-HOLE GOLF COURSE

Over the years, there have been several golf courses in the Estes Valley, including one in Moraine Park before it was part of Rocky Mountain National Park. Lake Estes 9-Hole Golf Course is for those wanting to play golf for the first time, those looking for a shorter game, or folks who prefer to play in the off-season surrounded by mountain views. Located on the northwest side of Lake Estes, the 9-hole golf course is mostly open year-round (weather permitting, with short closures in April and May for maintenance and in September for the elk rut). Come out to the course during September and you just might find a bull elk chasing his harem through the course.

690 Big Thompson Ave., 970-586-8176
golfestes.com

TIP

Estes Valley Recreation and Park District, which manages the two golf courses, have professional golfers on staff. If you have never played golf, consider hiring one of the pros to teach you the basics, including chipping, putting, and driving. If you know the sport but don't have your clubs, rent them at the pro shops located at each golf course.

WARM UP
WITH A SHORT HIKE
IN ROCKY MOUNTAIN NATIONAL PARK

There are more than 350 miles of trails in Rocky Mountain National Park—from the short, easy hikes around alpine lakes (see #56) to multi-day backpacking trips that will take you miles away from any modern conveniences. Most visitors, however, want to experience the park while still having time to be home for a barbecue dinner on the deck of their vacation rental. There are three short hikes that will each take you to a waterfall, two short hikes that take you to alpine lakes, and three that provide an alpine experience on the tundra. For waterfalls, hike out to Alberta Falls along Bear Lake Road, Adams Falls near Grand Lake along the East Inlet Trail, or Chasm Falls along Old Fall River Road. All three hikes are 1.5 miles or fewer in length. To reach the alpine lakes, check out the hike to Dream Lake above Bear Lake (bonus: you pass Nymph Lake on this trail; see #71 for additional information about Dream Lake) or Bierstadt Lake along Bear Lake Road. Each is slightly longer than one mile and does have some elevation gain but the views of Hallett and other nearby peaks make it worth the while. For a tundra experience, check out the Tundra Communities Trail from Rock Cut or Ute Trail across from the Alpine Visitor Center.

Rocky Mountain National Park: nps.gov/romo
Trail Ridge Road Status Line: 970-586-1222

PHOTOGRAPH LONGS PEAK,
THE TALLEST MOUNTAIN IN NORTHERN COLORADO

Colorado is home to 54 fourteeners, mountains that exceed 14,000 feet in elevation. The northernmost fourteener is Longs Peak, Rocky Mountain National Park's tallest mountain. This peak can be seen from most places in the park, and with each view, the appearance of the mountain changes just slightly—from the square-top profile seen from Trail Ridge Road to the Diamond seen on the eastern face along Colorado Highway 7. Because of the rounded top of Longs Peak, it works for sunrise and sunset photographs. The best spots are in the pullout along Colorado Highway 7 near the Salvation Army Camp, Lily Lake, Bear Lake, Beaver Meadows Overlook, Rock Cut, and Gore Range Overlook. The last two are located along Trail Ridge Road.

Rocky Mountain National Park: nps.gov/romo
Trail Ridge Road Status Line: 970-586-1222

TIP

Reaching the summit of 14,259-foot Longs Peak is a technical mountaineering climb, not a hike. It is an altogether different challenge and it is best not to attempt this mountain if you are not experienced with mountaineering. It is a difficult mountain to summit, taking about 10 hours to complete because it involves climbing about 5,000 feet in elevation over 13.5 miles. If you are interested in climbing Longs Peak, consider hiring a guide to talk you through what to expect and lead you on the adventure.

GO SLEDDING
AT HIDDEN VALLEY

The majority of people visit Rocky Mountain National Park in summer and early fall but this high-altitude park can also be a fun place to vacation during the winter. Although winter in Estes Park is no longer the snowy experience it once was, there is certainly plenty for snow-loving enthusiasts to do in the area, thanks to the high elevation of the surrounding mountains. One family-friendly spot to check out is Hidden Valley. Once home to the Hidden Valley Ski Area, which opened in 1955 and closed in 1991, this forested bowl within Rocky Mountain National Park welcomes backcountry skiers and snowshoers as well as kids of all ages looking to enjoy the snow on a sled. Rocky Mountain National Park keeps the former "bunny slopes" of the ski area open for sledding—the only area in the park where sledding is permitted—when snow conditions allow. Only plastic sleds are permitted (sleds can be rented in Estes Park). There is also a warming hut (open on weekends and holidays) and a heated restroom between the parking lot and sledding hill, all built from the original decommissioned lodge of Hidden Valley Ski Area.

Rocky Mountain National Park
970-586-1206
nps.gov/romo/planyourvisit/planning-for-a-winter-visit.htm

SNOWSHOE AND SLED RENTALS

Estes Park Mountain Shop
2050 Big Thompson Ave., 970-586-6548
estesparkmountainshop.com

Scot's Sporting Goods
870 Moraine Ave., 970-586-2877
scotssportinggoods.com

CRUISE THE SIGHTS
ALONG OLD FALL RIVER ROAD

Opened in 1920, Old Fall River Road was the original access route to the high country in Rocky Mountain National Park. After Trail Ridge Road was constructed and opened in 1932, Old Fall River Road became a one-way, car-accessible, nature trail. Drivers navigate the 9.4 miles of dirt road and switchbacks along the south-facing side of Mount Chapin through thick forest, past waterfalls, and into the alpine tundra, ending at Fall River Pass at 11,796 feet. Look for forest and tundra animals along the route, including black bears, moose, elk, mule deer, yellow-bellied marmots, snowshoe hares, and dusky grouse. There are no guardrails along the road and the steep drop-offs will make your heart skip a beat, but the adrenaline rush is well worth the experience. Remember this is a one-way road so once you start, you are committed to finishing. The road ends at the parking lot for the Alpine Visitor Center. You can return to Estes Park or Grand Lake by taking Trail Ridge Road back to town. This is a seasonal road, opening in early July and closing in early October. Vehicles longer than 25 feet in length and vehicles with trailers are prohibited.

Rocky Mountain National Park
970-586-1206
nps.gov/romo/planyourvisit/old_fall_river_road.htm

LOOK FOR BIGHORN SHEEP
IN THE BIG THOMPSON CANYON

Rocky Mountain National Park is loaded with a wide variety of wildlife, including bighorn sheep, but if you do not have the time to explore this large park, do not have a timed-entry reservation, or just want to check out a different spot for wildlife, take a drive down the scenic Big Thompson Canyon. Spanning 20 miles along US Highway 34 between Estes Park and Loveland, this canyon is home to more than 70 bighorn sheep. Although most of the year wildlife viewers will see herds of ewes (females), yearlings, and lambs in the canyon, there are also rams (males), which are more typically near the road during the fall rut. Bighorn sheep are Colorado's state mammal, the symbol for Colorado Parks and Wildlife, and an all-around icon of the Rocky Mountains. Agile and surefooted on the rocky slopes where they live, the sheep spend evenings in the higher elevations away from predators and then come down midday to eat and drink from the Big Thompson River. To find the sheep, look on the south-facing slope (the left side as you head down the canyon from Estes Park) for their white butts, which contrast with the dark, rocky slopes of the canyon walls. This is a busy highway so use designated pullouts to safely view the sheep.

Colorado Parks and Wildlife
cpw.state.co.us/learn/pages/speciesprofiles.aspx

LEARN A NEW ANGLE
FROM A LOCAL FLY-FISHING GUIDE

What better way to relax in Estes Park than fishing along one of the various rivers or lakes in the region? If you have never experienced fly fishing or are not familiar with fishing in the Rocky Mountains, hire an experienced guide from Kirks Flyshop or Estes Angler. With access to fishing hotspots in Rocky Mountain National Park, Estes Valley, and the Big Thompson River, there is sure to be a great day ahead on a pristine waterway surrounded by mountain peaks. Trips range from two-hour-long excursions to multi-day backpacking adventures. River float trips down the Colorado River are also available from Kirks Flyshop. Trips are conducted rain or shine, and include rod, reel, waders, and flies.

Kirks Flyshop
230 E Elkhorn Ave., Unit B, 970-577-0790
kirksflyshop.com

Estes Angler
338 W Riverside Dr., 970-586-2110
estesangler.com

WATCH SUNRISE FROM CENTENNIAL OPEN SPACE
AT KNOLL-WILLOWS

You could find a different spot to watch sunrise every day of the year near Estes Park and never duplicate the experience. Whether the cloud colors change, new weather rolls in, or you find a different angle of view, this is one of the prettiest places in the US to enjoy the calm, peaceful moments at sunrise. One of the best places to access with little effort is right in downtown Estes Park at the Birch Ruins at Centennial Open Space at Knoll-Willows. Located along East Wonderview Avenue across from the Stanley Hotel, a short one-quarter mile trail leads you to the Birch Ruins on the west side of the natural area. From here, you have a wide-open view of the Continental Divide, including Longs Peak and downtown Estes Park, perfect for a morning viewing of the Rocky Mountains as they turn from shades of purple to orange with the rising sun. Knoll-Willows is open year-round and there is no fee to access the 20 acres of open space.

Centennial Open Space at Knoll-Willows
larimer.gov/naturalresources/openlands/acquisitions/knoll-willows

HIKE THE
KRUGER ROCK TRAIL
IN HERMIT PARK OPEN SPACE

Although many people will consider Rocky Mountain National Park to be the only place in the Estes Park area to hike, there are actually many trails outside of the park for exploring that don't require a timed-entry reservation. One of those trails is Kruger Rock Trail in the 1,362-acre Hermit Park Open Space. Located about 2.5 miles southeast of Estes Park at an elevation of about 8,000 to 9,000 feet, Hermit Park Open Space is a secluded oasis close to town. Open from March through mid-December (when it closes seasonally for wintering elk), this open space has three trails, including the four-mile, out-and-back, Kruger Rock Trail with an elevation gain of 977 feet. From the top of Kruger Rock, hikers have views of Estes Park, Longs Peak, and the Continental Divide. Bonus: Dogs are permitted on this trail. Hermit Park has an entrance fee separate of the fee for Rocky Mountain National Park. The open space also offers RV and tent camping along with cabins for rent.

Hermit Park Open Space
970-577-2090
larimer.gov/naturalresources/parks/hermit-park

CAMP UNDER THE STARS
AT ONE OF FIVE CAMPGROUNDS IN
ROCKY MOUNTAIN NATIONAL PARK

There are certainly plenty of lodging options in Estes Park—
from high-end resorts to dispersed camping in the national
forest. But what better way to enjoy the Rocky Mountains than
to pitch a tent and sleep in the cool mountain air in Rocky
Mountain National Park. Really want to experience the park at
night? Reserve a campsite at Moraine Park during September so
you can hear the elk bugle all night long. It is truly a humbling
experience to be a part of this annual fall ritual. The park has five
campgrounds: Longs Peak, Aspenglen, Glacier Basin, Moraine
Park, and Timber Creek. All but Longs Peak require reservations,
and Timber Creek is the only campground on the west side of
the park. Moraine Park is the only campground that stays open
year-round. Reservations are released six months prior to your
camping date.

Rocky Mountain National Park
877-444-6777
nps.gov/romo/planyourvisit/camping.htm
Reservations: recreation.gov

WATCH THE ELK RUT
IN ESTES VALLEY

Estes Valley is home to more than 2,400 elk. Nothing represents autumn in the Rockies more than the sound of bugling male elk as they return to the mountain meadows in the park and in town during their annual fall mating season. Referred to as the rut, this season is marked by large bulls (males) wooing cows (females) with their high-pitched scream called a bugle, adorning their antlers with vegetation to create headdresses, spreading their scent on trees by rubbing them with their antlers, and creating wallows with their urine and then using the mud on their bodies like a high-end cologne. Satellite bulls try to encourage cows out of the harem, only to be chased off by the dominant bull. Evenly matched dominant bulls will square off with each other for a chance to show off their prowess to the cows. These displays of size and strength sometimes result in all-out battles that often end with one bull injured, or on rare occasions, dead. Ultimately, the cows choose their mates during this whole process, and the calves, well, they just try to stay out of the way. Since most mammals are more private about their mating rituals, this experience is unique for the opportunity to view it publicly from a back deck or restaurant window.

Season Itinerary

- Late August: the first bugles begin
- Early September: harems start to form with a dominant bull
- Last two weeks of September and first week of October: peak mating season
- End of October: bulls move back into bachelor herds and cows, yearlings (including those sad spikes who missed their moms), and calves form back into larger herds as the rut season winds down

Where

- In Estes Park: Stanley Park, Lake Estes 9-Hole Golf Course, Estes Park 18-Hole Golf Course, Wapiti Meadows, around Lake Estes, and on pretty much any street in town so be sure to check around corners and listen for the bugles
- In Rocky Mountain National Park:
  - East side: Horseshoe Park, Endovalley, Upper Beaver Meadows, and Moraine Park
  - West side: Holzwarth Meadows, Harbison Meadows, and Colorado River Trailhead area

How

- View from a distance. Elk do not like being in selfies. Maintain 25 yards (about two bus lengths) or more between you and the elk. Back away if an elk approaches you, do not drop your head towards a bull as if bending down (it is seen as a sign of aggression; trust me on this one), and do not get between a bull and the cows as his goal is to herd them back together if they wander off. He won't stop if you are in the way.
- Elk are most active in early morning and late afternoon.
- Be courteous of others. Do not stop in the middle of the road, leave car doors open, or make unexpected turns. Follow instructions in the park, including not entering meadows between 5 p.m. and 10 a.m. from September 1 to October 31 and park in designated parking lots and pullouts.
- Stay quiet while you enjoy the viewing to enhance the experience for all and reduce disturbing the wildlife.
- Give them room. Use a zoom lens.

TAKE FIDO
ON A DOG-FRIENDLY HIKE

Although dogs are permitted in parking and picnic areas in Rocky Mountain National Park, they are not permitted on any trails in the park. There are, however, plenty of dog-friendly hikes in the area—16 within 10 miles of the park—as well as a few other fun spots for your canine friend to enjoy the mountains with you. One of the most popular is the Estes Valley Dog Park located at Stanley Park. With two areas for dogs to play, including one dedicated to small or shy dogs, there is plenty of space to exercise your pet, including an obstacle course and swimming in the lake. A portion of the Fish Creek Trail navigates through Stanley Park, which connects to the Lake Estes Trail, both of which are dog friendly. Roosevelt National Forest surrounds Estes Park to the east and south. Here, dogs on leash are welcome and hikers can find trails for all skill levels. Some of the closest and most popular are Lily Mountain Trail, Lion Gulch Trail, and Panorama Peak. Another spot to check out is Hermit Park Open Space, where the Kruger Rock Trail is a divine destination for you and your canine hiking partner. (See #67 for additional information about the Kruger Rock Trail.)

Estes Valley Dog Park
Corner of Community Dr. and US Hwy. 36, 970-586-8191
evrpd.com

Roosevelt National Forest
970-295-6600
fs.usda.gov/arp

Hermit Park Open Space
970-577-2090
larimer.gov/naturalresources/parks/hermit-park

HIKE TO DREAM LAKE
FOR SUNRISE

Many destinations in Rocky Mountain National Park—from easy, short, half-mile walks to strenuous multi-hour treks—are ideal for watching a sunrise. Much of the park faces east so the peaks welcome the morning sun by reflecting glowing shades of pink, purple, and orange as the sun rises in the east. For a short but moderate trail (because of its elevation) to watch sunrise, hike to Dream Lake. The 2.2-mile roundtrip trail starts at 9,449-foot Bear Lake, passes lily pad-covered Nymph Lake, and ends at 9,905-foot Dream Lake, where this alpine jewel sits below the 12,720-foot-high Hallett Peak. Enjoy this trail any time of the year, with summer being the most popular. Although winter is an amazing time to visit this blue and white scene of frozen water and snow, be aware that the area can be prone to avalanches and the trail will be icy and snow-packed. The drive to the Bear Lake parking lot is about 45 minutes from Estes Park and requires the option one timed-entry reservation for the Bear Lake Road Corridor between 5 a.m. and 6 p.m. from Memorial Day Weekend to the second Monday in October. No reservation is required outside of this time frame. If you want to watch or photograph sunrise at Dream Lake, plan an hour for the hike to be sure you reach the water's edge in time for the best light—about 10 to 15 minutes before sunrise. Hike with a headlamp as the trail passes through thick forest, which will be dark in the early morning.

nps.gov/thingstodo/romo_dreamlake.htm

TEE OFF
AT ONE OF THE OLDEST GOLF COURSES IN COLORADO

Incorporated in 1917 and built on the former golf course of Lord Dunraven, the founding board of the Estes Park 18-Hole Golf Course included some of Estes Park's most influential men. High on that list are Julian Hayden, a civil engineer in Estes Park, whose name was given to Mount Julian in Rocky Mountain National Park and Enoch J. Mills, brother of Enos Mills, the "father of Rocky Mountain National Park." The Estes Park 18-Hole Golf Course has seen a lot of changes in the Estes Valley in its 100-plus years, including being converted to a nine-hole golf course in the 1930s so an airstrip could be built on its western edge. The airstrip was closed in the late 1940s due to its dangerous location in the valley. With views of Longs Peak, this course is considered one of the prettiest in the country— ranked the sixth most beautiful golf course in the US in *The Golf Book of Lists*—and is one of few where you might have to play through a herd of elk. The course is open from mid-April to October 31, weather permitting.

1480 Golf Course Rd., 970-586-8146
evrpd.com

EXPLORE THE YMCA OF THE ROCKIES CAMPUS
WITH A DAY PASS

At more than 860 acres, YMCA of the Rockies is one of the largest YMCA campuses in the US and their list of activities exemplifies why. With fun things to do like roller skating (the only place to do so in Estes Park), an indoor pool, mini golf, dog park, disc golf, basketball, tennis, axe throwing, horseback riding, escape room, archery, and more, there is sure to be something for every member of the family to enjoy. Not a guest? No problem. Just purchase a day pass. Some activities do require an additional fee with the day pass and guests of the YMCA of the Rockies do have priority for reservations.

2515 Tunnel Rd., 970-586-3341
ymcarockies.org

TIP

This vast campus includes lodges and cabins for up to 4,700 guests. Even with that many beds, this popular facility books quickly because of its capacity for accommodating large groups. If you would like to stay here to take advantage of the various amenities, have priority for activity reservations, and/or enjoy its off-the-beaten path location, book early or visit in a shoulder season like May or October.

The Stanley Hotel

CULTURE
AND HISTORY

TAKE THE GHOST TOUR
AT THE STANLEY HOTEL

Stephen King and his wife stayed at the Stanley Hotel in 1974 in Room 217 as the only guests in the hotel. It was the end of the season and the staff was closing the hotel but graciously let them stay. That visit and the haunting dream he had while there gave him ideas for the plot of his best-selling novel and subsequent movie, *The Shining*. King hasn't been the only person to get a sense of dread while in the hotel. Hotel guests, staff, and visitors stepping foot into the 140-room Georgian Colonial Revival–style hotel, which opened in 1909, have reported supernatural events, disembodied voices, phantom touches by something they can't see, and other unexplainable occurrences. Several television shows, including *Ghost Hunters*, have filmed episodes here to discuss theories of the hotel's hauntings. Not a believer? Take one of the hotel's spirits tours to see if you have a firsthand experience of orbs in photos or soft wisps of wind in your ears.

333 Wonderview Ave., 970-577-4000
stanleyhotel.com

VISIT
THE HISTORIC ELKHORN LODGE

The historic Elkhorn Lodge holds a lot of history for Estes Park. The late 19th century-style hunting lodge was originally established as a ranch where William and Ella James raised cattle as far back as 1874. Situated along Fall River with easy access to Horseshoe Park for cattle grazing, the Jameses offered their lodge as a place for summer guests to stay. They found that their guesthouse operation was more profitable than ranching in the unforgiving mountains. In addition to being one of the first ranches in the region, it was also home to the first golf course, the first school, and the first church in Estes Park, and is considered to be the oldest continuously operating hotel in Colorado. Sold to a developer in 2021, the updated property will continue to maintain the rustic tradition with modern amenities and expanded restaurant and lodging options. Listed on the National and State Registers of Historic Places, Elkhorn Lodge represents a unique part of Estes Park's early history when wildlife roamed the valleys, rivers flowed free, and traffic jams were still decades away.

600 Elkhorn Ave., 970-586-4416
elkhornlodge.org

LEARN ABOUT THE ALVA B. ADAMS TUNNEL
THAT RUNS BELOW THE CONTINENTAL DIVIDE

Water is a precious resource in the West. The growing population of Colorado and other Western states receive their water—sourced from snowpack high in the mountains—from reservoirs located throughout this region. But have you ever thought about how that water gets to the faucet in your home? The Alva B. Adams Tunnel is one of the methods. Built between 1940 and 1944 as part of the 250-mile Colorado-Big Thompson Project, the 13.1-mile, 10-foot-wide, concrete-lined Adams Tunnel is the largest water-diversion project in Colorado, moving water from the Colorado River on the west side of Rocky Mountain National Park to the east side. Today, the project collects, stores, and delivers more than 200,000 acre-feet of water each year to more than one million people and 615,000 acres of irrigated farmland. There are several interpretive signs around Estes Park with information about the project and the tunnel, including those at Lake Estes and East Portal at the end of Tunnel Road. The Bureau of Reclamation and Northern Water collaborate to manage the Colorado-Big Thompson Project.

Northern Water: northern water.org/what-we-do/deliver-water/
colorado-big-thompson-project

Bureau of Reclamation: usbr.gov/projects/index.php?id=432

TOUR THE CABIN MUSEUM
OF ENOS MILLS, THE "FATHER OF ROCKY MOUNTAIN NATIONAL PARK"

Born to a poor family in Kansas in 1870, Enos Mills came to Colorado several times before he finally saved enough money to buy land and build a cabin in 1885 at the base of Longs Peak. A guide during the summer months, Mills loved the area and thoroughly explored it, climbing Longs Peak an astounding 297 times. Although Mills never went to school, he was intrigued by the natural world and pursued his interests in his leisure time. After a fire destroyed a mine where he worked during the winter months in Montana, Mills traveled around the country, staying in California for several weeks. During this time, he met conservationist John Muir. It was this friendship with Muir that spurred Mills's desire to become a conservationist and fight to save the land that would become Rocky Mountain National Park. Today, Mills's original cabin has become a quaint museum that showcases his achievements. Tours are by appointment only. Call ahead to schedule a time.

6760 Colorado Hwy. 7, 970-586-4706
enosmills.com/brochure.html

EXPLORE A HISTORIC, WORKING RANCH
AT THE MACGREGOR RANCH MUSEUM

Established in 1873 by Alexander and Clara MacGregor, the MacGregor Ranch is nestled in the beautiful Black Canyon Creek area of Estes Park. Preserved in a trust after the 1970 death of Muriel MacGregor, the third generation to own the property, the ranch has been forever preserved as a working cattle ranch and a youth education center. Housed in the original main ranch home, the museum takes visitors back into history at one of the finest examples of an early homestead ranch in Colorado. A tour includes three generations of furnishings, family memorabilia and historic photos, a self-guided walking tour of a blacksmith shop and smokehouse, and spectacular views of Lumpy Ridge and the surrounding meadows. The museum is open Tuesday through Saturday in June, July, and August. Contact the museum for tours at other times of the year.

180 MacGregor Ln., 970-586-3749
macgregorranch.org

ENJOY
AWARD-WINNING ART
AT THE OLD GALLERY

Located about 15 miles south of Estes Park in the small town of Allenspark, The Old Gallery is a community gathering place for the mountain towns along Colorado Highway 7, including Allenspark, Raymond, Riverside, and Estes Park. Home to more than 30 artists, this eclectic gallery represents some of Colorado's finest artwork, including jewelry, photography, sculpture, paintings, stained glass, and more. Originally built in 1904 as part of the Rubendall family homestead, The Old Gallery has been used for a wide variety of purposes, including a full-time home, a summer cabin, a rental property, a general store, an antique shop, and an ATV rental business. All of these various uses left the building needing substantial renovations and in 2008, the Allenspark Community Cultures Council formed to buy the building and create a gallery and community center. After major renovations, The Old Gallery reopened in 2015.

14863 Colorado Hwy. 7, Allenspark, 303-747-2906
theoldgallery.org

UNLOCK THE MYSTERIES
OF THE WORLD'S LARGEST KEY
COLLECTION AT THE SEVEN KEYS LODGE

There are many unique collections throughout the US: the largest ball of twine, a hammer museum, and the largest collection of Pez dispensers, just to name a few. Estes Park is no exception, being home to the world's largest collection of keys—more than 20,000. Located at the Seven Keys Lodge (formerly the Baldpate Inn), this collection will take you on a unique tour of some of the world's most famous homes, buildings, and businesses. The collection includes a key to the White House, Frankenstein's Castle, Westminster Abbey, Mozart's wine cellar, and Adolf Hitler's bunker. Keys to less well-known locations with equally interesting stories include robbed banks and dressing rooms of Hollywood actors. Seven Keys Lodge, a small bed and breakfast on Colorado Highway 7 across from Lily Lake, was built in 1917 by Ethel and Gordon Mace. They named it after a hotel from the novel, *The Seven Keys to Baldpate*, where seven guests were each given "the only" key to the hotel to visit it in the winter. They all show up with different agendas, creating a mystery to be solved. The Mace's liked the idea and handed out keys for their own Estes Park hotel until metal costs hindered the effort. Instead, guests started bringing their own keys and a collection began to form.

4900 Colorado Hwy. 7, 970-586-5397
sevenkeyslodge.com

SEE
A FRANK LLOYD
WRIGHT–INSPIRED BUILDING

Frank Lloyd Wright is one of the most well-known American architects, having designed 1,114 architectural works of all types over seven decades. His designs changed how we build and live in innovative spaces using a concept he called "organic architecture." This design technique celebrated the environment by designing structures that fit their landscapes. Some of his most famous buildings, like Fallingwater, where a waterfall is incorporated into the home, illustrated this concept. In Estes Park, the Beaver Meadows Visitor Center was designed by Tom Casey, a mentee of Frank Lloyd Wright, who worked at the architectural firm Taliesin Associated Architects. This firm was founded by Wright's apprentices after his death in 1959 to carry on his organic design style. Completed in 1967, eight years after Wright's death, the Beaver Meadows's building integrates materials native to the area. It also appears to be a single-story building but, in keeping with Wright's design style, is actually two stories nestled into the sloping terrain. The building houses Rocky Mountain National Park's administrative offices as well as a gift shop, memorials for various people associated with the park, the information desk, and an amphitheater.

Beaver Meadows Visitor Center
1000 US Hwy. 36, 970-586-1206
nps.gov/romo/planyourvisit/visitorcenters.htm

WALK BACK IN TIME
AT ESTES PARK'S ORIGINAL
POWER PLANT

The Stanley Hotel, named for the genius inventor, entrepreneur, and hotelier, wasn't the only thing that F. O. Stanley built in Estes Park. He also established a sewer service, an electric company, and a power plant. He built distribution lines throughout Estes Park so other residents could purchase electricity and installed wooden pipes for a water distribution system in town. The Historic Fall River Hydroplant, located near the Fall River entrance to Rocky Mountain National Park, was built in 1909 to produce electricity for the Stanley Hotel. Rare for hotels in the mountains at the time, electric light and water from the tap greeted guests arriving on opening day. Stanley, however, was used to modern conveniences after living his first 50 years in New England and wanted to bring them with him to Estes Park. The hydroplant, built three miles northwest of Estes Park, is a one-story, concrete-floored 28 by 26-square-foot building that houses a turbine and a 200-kilowatt generator. Water from nearby Cascade Lake powered the turbine. The hydroplant operated successfully until the Lawn Lake Flood of 1982 damaged its equipment. The hydroplant is now open for tours Wednesdays through Saturdays from June 1 to September 30.

1754 Fish Hatchery Rd., 970-586-6256
estespark.Colorado.gov/departments/museum/plan-a-visit

● ●

TAKE A WALKING TOUR OF THE BIRCH RUINS AT CENTENNIAL OPEN SPACE
AT KNOLL-WILLOWS

Estes Park was a fledgling town when the Birch bungalow was built. Only a few buildings existed in downtown Estes Park: a post office, a community building, a store, and John Cleave's house. At the age of 22, Albert "Al" Birch, a city editor and publicity manager at the *Denver Post*, purchased the rocky ridge that is now Centennial Open Space at Knoll-Willows. He built a one-story stone house with views of Longs Peak, the Continental Divide, and the growing town of Estes Park. The year was 1905. On December 21, 1907, the building burned, leaving only the stone walls, iron frame, and the fireplace where the blaze started. A few years later, Birch built a smaller, wooden cabin on the property, which was used by his family as a summer retreat until the town of Estes Park bought the property in the 1980s. These features and the history behind them are explained during walking tours given each summer by docents of the Estes Park Museum. The wooden cabin is only open to the public during the docent-led tours, but the grounds and ruins are open to the public year-round.

170 MacGregor Ave., 970-586-6256
estespark.colorado.gov/departments/museum/plan-a-visit

LEARN THE RICH HISTORY OF ESTES VALLEY
AT THE ESTES PARK MUSEUM

This small mountain town has a rich history that's different from most mountain towns in Colorado. Most settlers came to Colorado to ranch or take their chances at mining. Mines were sparce in the mountains surrounding Estes Valley with only about 80 recorded in Rocky Mountain National Park. Ranching was attempted but winter winds and dry habitat make this area a difficult place to raise animals or the crops to feed them. Early settlers, like Lord Dunraven, saw Estes Valley as a hunting paradise full of bighorn sheep, elk, and mule deer. As a result, the region became more of a recreation mecca where outdoor enthusiasts, including hunters, fishermen, artists, and explorers, could escape from the crowds and pollution of the growing Front Range towns to the cool, clean mountain air. Learn about the history of Estes Park, including its interesting characters like Isabella Bird, Enos Mills, F. O. Stanley, Albert Bierstadt, Joel Estes, and many others, through the museum's extensive collection of 30,000 objects and interactive displays. The original headquarters building for Rocky Mountain National Park is also on the museum property. The museum is free and open year-round from Wednesday to Saturday.

200 4th St., 970-586-6256
estespark.colorado.gov/museum

MEET THE STANLEYS
AT THE STANLEY HOME MUSEUM

F. O. Stanley and his wife, Flora, arrived in Estes Park in June 1903 so that the clean mountain air could help F. O. overcome his struggle with tuberculosis. The house, built in 1904 to the west of their iconic hotel, remained their summer home until his death in 1940. During their time in Estes Park, they were responsible for helping the town transform from a fledgling mountain town to a bustling tourist destination. With their tremendous wealth and modern East Coast style, they brought conveniences to Estes Valley, like improved roads, a power and electric company, water distribution, the first bank, and a transportation company for visitors. Flora's influence created the Estes Park Woman's Club and local service groups to help establish a national park, support schools and settlement houses for low-income women, and much more. Learn about this interesting couple and their continuing impact on Estes Park by visiting the Stanley Home Museum.

415 W Wonderview Ave., 970-235-0062
stanleyhome.org

WALK IN THE FOOTSTEPS OF A POPE
AT CHAPEL ON THE ROCK
AT CAMP ST. MALO

Many people find the comfort of the outdoors to be as empowering and spiritual as being in a church. It is therefore no wonder that Colorado's mountain valleys are filled with religious retreats, remote churches, and sacred landmarks. One of the most stunning of these religious centers is Saint Catherine of Siena Chapel, also known as Chapel on the Rock. Located on Colorado Highway 7 in Allenspark, the church is believed to be the only such building in Colorado to have been blessed by a pope. In 1993, Pope John Paul II visited the chapel at the Catholic retreat center as part of the World Youth Day event and blessed the chapel during his stay. The structure looks like something out of a medieval story set in Old World England with its mix of Romanesque Revival and European medieval styles although it was actually completed in 1936. Visitors can tour the chapel Tuesday to Sunday from 10 a.m. to 4 p.m. Masses are held every Friday at 8:30 a.m., and weddings are still celebrated at the church as well.

10758 Colorado Hwy. 7, Allenspark; 303-747-2786
campstmalo.org

EXPLORE LOCAL NATIVE AMERICAN HISTORY AND ART
AT EAGLE PLUME'S INDIAN TRADING POST

A nondescript log cabin with a feather-shaped sign is tucked into the ponderosa forest on the east side of Colorado Highway 7 and holds a representative collection of Indian art and culture. Established in 1917 as the What Not Inn, the shop sold antiques, art, and curios, and was decorated with some of the items from the shop owner's collection of Lakota beadwork. Renamed Perkins Trading Post after shop owner Katherine Lindsay married O. S. Perkins, Charles Eagle Plume started helping her run the outlet and entertained visitors with his tribal lore and dancing, sometimes wearing full Native American regalia. Eagle Plume became the owner after Lindsay's death and has continued to perform and lecture about Native American art and culture. The post has more than one thousand historic and prehistoric pieces from Native North America, Alaska, and Canada, and sells contemporary works in jewelry, textiles, basketry, beadwork, and more.

9853 Colorado Hwy. 7, Allenspark; 303-747-2861
eagle-plumes.com

DIG INTO GEOLOGY
AT THE HISTORIC DICK'S ROCK MUSEUM

Heading back to town along Moraine Avenue after a day in Rocky Mountain National Park, you may notice a large shop surrounded by boulders of all shapes, sizes, and colors. This is Dick's Rock Museum, located inside of the Red Rose Rock Shop. Step inside and your visual senses will be overwhelmed by the mélange of color in the large collection of rocks and polished stones. Shelves are filled with black, pink, purple, red, and white samples of one of Earth's hardest substances. Check out Dick's collection, housed in a smaller portion of the building but full of unique finds like the tooth of a wooly mammoth, a sample of rocks from as far away as Germany and India, and a collection of crazy lace agate from Mexico. Don't leave without trying your hand at panning outside the main entrance. Want a piece of Colorado for your home? Purchase one of the large boulders made of peridot, rhyolite, selenite, or rose quartz in the shop's yard. Looking for something a little smaller? Go with a fossil or polished stone bookends.

490 Moraine Ave., 970-586-4180
redroserockshopestes.com

RESERVE THE FOURTH EARL OF DUNRAVEN'S
ORIGINAL CABIN

When Irish aristocrat Windham Thomas Wyndham-Quinn, the Fourth Earl of Dunraven, first entered Estes Valley on December 27, 1872, he found an untouched landscape and immediately became entranced with the hunting opportunities in this mountain valley. He returned in 1873 and 1874 with a plan to acquire all of Estes Valley for a private hunting preserve. In 1877, on the advice of his friend, the Western painter Albert Bierstadt, Dunraven built a hotel. The Estes Park Hotel, also known as the "English" hotel, was an instant success but the Earl of Dunraven started to lose interest in Estes Valley and had his last visit in the mid-1880s. He sold his land to F. O. Stanley and B. D. Sanborn in 1908. Although the Estes Park Hotel burned down in 1911, the Dunraven Cottage, which was built in 1876, still stands at its original location on Fish Creek Road on the east side of Estes Park. The cottage can be reserved through SkyRun Estes Park Vacation Rentals by those looking to experience a piece of Estes Park's history firsthand.

890 Fish Creek Rd., 970-235-5550
estespark.skyrun.com

The Taffy Shop

SHOPPING
AND FASHION

CELEBRATE CHRISTMAS ALL YEAR LONG
AT THE CHRISTMAS SHOPPE AND THE SPRUCE HOUSE

Estes Park is a quiet town around the holidays. Although this mountain community continues to expand winter recreation opportunities, most people visit late spring to early fall. So, experience a little Christmas-in-July by stopping in these fun shops. For five decades, visitors and locals alike have purchased beautiful holiday decorations from these shops and taken them home to relive their Estes Park experience at the holidays year after year. But it isn't just the adorable fishing and hunting themed ornaments or the red-and-green-dressed bears and moose that make these shops a must for return visits. The Spruce House is located in a 100-year-old home, giving this shop the feel of an early 20th-century Christmas. In keeping with this theme, the shop carries Annalee Dolls, Byers Carolers, and Department 56 Village items. And if collectibles and displays are not your thing, just stop in either shop to pick up a Colorado-themed, year-round home decoration in the shape of Longs Peak, elk, or hiking boots.

The Christmas Shoppe
330 E Elkhorn Ave., 970-586-2882
thechristmasshops.com

The Spruce House
125 Spruce Dr., 970-586-2882
thechristmasshops.com

WATCH GLASSBLOWING
IN DOWNTOWN ESTES PARK

When you think of glassblowing, images of Colonial Williamsburg may pop into your head long before you envision downtown Estes Park. Surprisingly, however, the town supports two glassworks galleries. Colorado is full of creative artists using any medium you can conjure up to create unique pieces, and the artists who started these galleries are no exception. It is believed the beauty of Colorado not only attracted artists to the Centennial State but keeps them here because of the constant inspiration. Each gallery has its own style. Mountain Blown Glass is more of a demonstration and custom-glass shop. Be sure to check out their hand-blown ornaments and the wedding piece service where the bride and groom can select colored glass chips to be made into a custom glass piece. Patterson Glassworks follows more of a traditional gallery style with glasses, dishware, and other decorative options to enhance any area of a home. Both galleries have active kilns so it is quite likely that shoppers will see glass pieces being made during the visit.

Patterson Glassworks
323 W Elkhorn Ave., 970-586-8619
glassworksofestespark.com

Mountain Blown Glass
101-A W Elkhorn Ave., 970-577-0880
mountainblownglass.net

BUY FRESH
AT THE WEEKLY SUMMER FARMERS MARKET

With a long history in farming and ranching, farmers markets bring out the best of Colorado's harvest. There are more than 100 farmers markets throughout the state but few have the views of the weekly Estes Valley Farmers Market. Held every Thursday morning from June through September, the market hosts more than 30 vendors bringing a wide variety of Colorado-made and Colorado-grown items: fruits, vegetables, fresh breads, plants, hanging baskets, floral arrangements, honey, coffee, beef, bison, cheese, freshly made tamales, baskets, and much more. And don't leave without picking up a bag of famous Colorado kettle corn, a local favorite for anyone with a sweet tooth. Although some vendors do accept credit cards, others only accept cash so best to have some currency on hand. The Farmers Market is held every Thursday morning at the Estes Park Visitor Center parking lot. Free parking is available at the Estes Park Parking Garage behind the visitor center.

500 Big Thompson Ave., 970-577-9900

ENJOY
SWEET, GOOEY SALTWATER TAFFY

For those who grew up on the East Coast, where saltwater taffy was born, it is more synonymous with boardwalks and fishing piers than cool mountain breezes and jagged peaks. In Estes Park, however, the gooey treat is a popular purchase with several stores in downtown Estes Park offering the melt-in-your-mouth dinner spoiler. The oldest continuously operating taffy concession in town is The Taffy Shop. Since 1935, visitors have enjoyed watching the taffy puller in the front window, including many who remember watching that same machine work its magic decades ago. Their taffy recipe still remains under lock and key but shoppers can enjoy its result, coming in flavors like cinnamon, peppermint, sea-salted caramel, lemon, Texas pecan, vanilla, molasses, and chocolate. Although many shops in Estes Park sell saltwater taffy, only two make the product here in town.

The Taffy Shop
121 W Elkhorn Ave., 970-586-4548
originaltaffyshop.com

Purple Mountain Taffy Co.
121 E Elkhorn Ave., 970-586-3407
purplemountaintaffy.com

FIND THE
PERFECT MEMENTO
AT TRENDZ

Walk Elkhorn Avenue, the main drag through Estes Park, any summer afternoon and you will be tempted to pop into dozens of trinket, T-shirt, souvenir, and novelty shops. Many have similar products and the repetition can become monotonous. For something unique to take home as a memento of your trip to the Rocky Mountains—whether that is from thousands of miles away or just a jaunt up the hill from the Front Range—stop in Trendz at the Park. Located at the corner of Elkhorn and Moraine, this shop caters to finding Colorado-themed gifts and home décor, and striving to constantly keep that inventory fresh. Not only do they go a step above in their product line, they also make a commitment to protect the natural environment—a worthy effort considering their location in one of the prettiest spots in the US—by participating in a variety of green initiatives.

100 E Elkhorn Ave., 970-577-0831

PICK OUT
THE BEST T-SHIRT TO
HIGHLIGHT YOUR VISIT
AT BROWNFIELD'S

Estes Park used to be a seasonal mountain town, with shops shuttering in late October just before the snows became constant enough to prevent visitors from comfortably strolling downtown. Today, Estes Park has transformed into a year-round destination with hikes to do in summer, snowshoe routes to finish in winter, and many places to shop all year long. One establishment, however, still stays true to its seasonal roots, and its commitment to the highest quality at the best prices. Brownfields, which opened in 1956 as a saddle and Western wear shop, creates a sense of urgency to get the latest and greatest Colorado or Rocky Mountain National Park-themed T-shirt, hat, or souvenir before the shop closes for the season. Periodically, the store is restocked with completely new inventory, giving visitors a reason to visit again and again when in Estes Park. If you happen to be in the area at the end of the summer season—typically in October—be sure to visit Brownfields for their end-of-season sale when everything must go.

350 E Elkhorn Ave., 970-586-3275
shopbrownfields.com

VISIT THE DOZEN ART GALLERIES
IN DOWNTOWN ESTES PARK

Colorado is home to thousands of talented artists—photographers, quilt makers, painters, jewelry designers, sculptors, and woodworkers. The cold winter nights and the boundless supply of inspiration make Colorado a haven for artists. Estes Park is no exception as proven by the large variety of galleries in town. Most are located in the downtown area but there are several worth visiting scattered throughout Estes Valley.

For the latest about Estes Park's thriving art scene and upcoming art shows, visit Estes Arts District at estesartsdistrict.org.

TIP

Beyond the galleries scattered throughout the area, Estes Park hosts a number of art markets from May through November. Some of the most popular include the Annual Art Market on Memorial Day Weekend, Estes Park Arts and Crafts Festival on Labor Day Weekend, and the Fine Arts and Crafts Festival in mid-September. For the latest list of events, see the calendar on Visit Estes Park's website (visitestespark.com/events-calendar).

Alpenglow Images and Accents
145 E Elkhorn Ave., #103
970-577-6802
alpenglowimages.info

Art Center of Estes Park
517 Big Thompson Ave.
970-586-5882
artcenterofestes.com

Aspen and Evergreen Gallery
356 E Elkhorn Ave., Unit 1
970-586-4355
aspenandevergreen.com

Don Van Horn Gallery
440 E Elkhorn Ave.
303-349-7049
donvanhorn.gallery

Earthwood Artisans
360 E Elkhorn Ave.
970-586-2151
earthwoodartisans.com

Earthwood Collections
141 E Elkhorn Ave.
970-577-8100
earthwoodgalleries.com

Estes Park Silver and Gold
145 E Elkhorn Ave., #105
970-443-4259
estesparksilve
randgold.com

Images of RMNP
203 Park Ln.
970-586-4352
imagesofrmnp.com

Mountain Blown Glass
101 W Elkhorn Ave.
970-577-0880
mountainblownglass.net

**Mystic Mountain
Gallery and Gifts**
410 E Elkhorn Ave.
970-586-1853
diankadesigns.com

The Old Gallery
14863 Colorado Hwy. 7
Allenspark, 303-747-2906
theoldgallery.org

**Patterson Glassworks
Studio and Gallery**
323 W Elkhorn Ave.
970-586-8619
glassworksofestespark.com

Wild Spirits Art Gallery
148 W Elkhorn Ave.
970-586-4392
wildspiritsgalleryestespark.com

Wynbrier Wildlife Gallery
238 E Elkhorn Ave.
970-586-4074
wynbrier.com

HIKE IN STYLE
WITH BOOTS FROM PLUM CREEK SHOE STATION

In some towns, finding the right hiking boots can be so difficult that shoppers resort to surfing the Web and buying a few pairs to try out before finding a style that works. In Estes Park, visitors and locals agree that Plum Creek Shoe Station is the best place to find just the right boots (or sandals, mountain casual shoes, or sneakers) for your outdoor adventure. With a staff trained to make sure you find properly fitting shoes in a style you like from their wide range of popular brands, Plum Creek Shoe Station goes above and beyond to make sure their customers are satisfied. Visit their sister store, Moose Creek, for the best Western wear in town.

Plum Creek
135 Moraine Ave., 970-586-4061
plumcreekshoes.com

Moose Creek
125 C Moraine Ave., 970-577-7463
moosecreekwestern.com

SHOP COLORADO-STYLE CLOTHING
AT HYK

When driving around Colorado you may notice the bumper stickers that resemble the green-and-white design of the state's license plates proclaiming "Colorado Native." Hyk exudes that Colorado-lifestyle vibe for all things outdoor. Owner and Director of Other Things, Ben Ferguson, is a Colorado native who wanted a single source shop for high-quality outdoor apparel, equipment, and footwear in Estes Park. Lifelong hikers of the Rocky Mountain National Park trails, Ferguson and his staff know what a hiker needs to stay comfortable and safe in the outdoors while looking stylish in the process. Stop in to see how they can help you bring the Rocky Mountain lifestyle to wherever you call home.

149 E Elkhorn Ave., 970-586-3200
hyklife.com

PICK UP ALL THE RIGHT OUTDOOR GEAR
AT SCOT'S SPORTING GOODS

When backpacking in Rocky Mountain National Park, hikers must carry a bear-proof container with them to store toiletries, food, and other scented items that might attract the curious bear. Although there are several options on the market, the only one that truly works is a bear canister. They can be heavy, expensive, and impractical for much else but when you need them to work, they work. To save hikers from buying a single-purpose item, Scot's Sporting Goods rents these for backpacking trips. But they don't just rent bear canisters; they are also a full-service, outdoor adventure shop offering rentable and new gear for many outdoor interests and guided trips. If traveling with your camping gear doesn't sound appealing, rent a camp stove, tent, and sleeping bags from Scot's. If you are looking to head to the local river for an afternoon of fishing, pick up your Colorado fishing license, tackle, and fishing hat at Scot's. They also rent hiking poles, snowshoes, kid carriers, daypacks, and backpacks. Hire one of their knowledgeable guides for a fly-fishing, hiking, or snowshoeing adventure. Before you leave, don't forget to stock up on the necessary supplies for a day in the mountains, like sunscreen, hiking clothes, fishing waders, and much, much more.

870 Moraine Ave., 970-586-2877
scotssportinggoods.com

• •

REACH YOUR SARTORIAL POTENTIAL
AT THE GREY HOUSE

Not everything in Estes Park is about taking a hike or going fishing. Estes Park also has several highly rated restaurants, and the mountain views attract many to the area for a weekend anniversary getaway, destination wedding, or other special occasion. If you are looking for an ensemble that is somewhere between that casual hiking look and formalwear, try the Grey House. Here, shoppers can browse the wide selection of upscale, mountain-style, trendy attire from well-known labels to unique artisan-made clothing, jewelry, and accessories. It is the ideal place to pick up an accent piece like a felt hat or Western-inspired sweater coat to add a little flair to an outfit. There are styles available for men, women, and children.

130 E Elkhorn Ave., 970-577-7000
thegreyhouse.boutique

ACTIVITIES
BY SEASON

WINTER

Pair Excellent Beer with Local Sound
  at the Rock Inn Mountain Tavern, 14

Enjoy Award-Winning Art at The Old Gallery, 101

Experience the Thrills of a Mountain Rollercoaster, 39

Shop Colorado-Style Clothing at Hyk, 123

Take a Class or Tour with Rocky Mountain Conservancy, 59

Dig into Geology at the Historic Dick's Rock Museum, 110

Play a Short Round of Golf at the Lake Estes 9-Hole Golf Course, 74

SPRING

Watch a Movie at the Oldest Single-Screen Movie Theater in the US, 52

Start Your Day with a Sunrise at Sprague Lake, 57

Take the Ghost Tour at the Stanley Hotel, 96

Hike in Style with Boots from Plum Creek Shoe Station, 122

Enjoy Sweet, Gooey Saltwater Taffy, 117

Hike to the Thumb in the Thumb Open Space, 56

Indulge in a Pizza from a World Champion Pizza Maker, 21

Hike up Trail Ridge Road Before the Road Opens to Cars, 65

SUMMER

FALL

• •

Rooftop Rodeo

SUGGESTED
ITINERARIES

DATERS

Indulge Yourself with Cherry Pie, Colorado Style, 2

Rent a Bike, Pedal Cart, Kayak, or Boat at Lake Estes Marina, 72

Pack a Lunch and Fishing Pole for a Picnic at Lake Estes, 6

Have a Date Night at Bird and Jim, 17

Enjoy a Slow Afternoon with a Glass of Wine at Snowy Peaks Winery, 5

Go Horseback Riding in the Rocky Mountains, 71

FOODIES

Get a Taste of Southern-Style Barbecue in the Mountain Air, 11

Try a Breakfast Platter at the Locals' Favorite Breakfast Restaurant, 19

Reward Yourself with a Donut Haus Dozen on the Way to Your Hike, 24

Savor the Biggest Cinnamon Rolls in Town Before They Are Gone, 15

Find Your Favorite Pie at the Best Dessert Place in Town, 16

Hook a Brew and Tasty Fish Filet at Lumpy Ridge Brewery, 8

Spoil Your Taste Buds with the Best Margarita in Town, 22

• •

HISTORY SEEKERS

MOUNTAIN CLIMBERS

● ●

KID-FRIENDLY ADVENTURES

SHOPAHOLICS

MUSIC LOVERS

• •

CREATIVE CHOICES

Enjoy Award-Winning Art at The Old Gallery, 101

Photograph Longs Peak, the Tallest Mountain in Northern Colorado, 76

Visit the Dozen Art Galleries in Downtown Estes Park, 120

Explore Local Native American History and Art at Eagle Plume's Indian Trading Post, 109

Capture a Sunset in Rocky Mountain National Park, 68

Watch Glassblowing in Downtown Estes Park, 115

OUTDOORS

View the Night Skies from 12,000 Feet, 69

Watch the Elk Rut in Estes Valley, 86

Play a Game of Disc Golf at One of Two Courses in Estes Park, 47

Learn a New Angle from a Local Fly-Fishing Guide, 82

Rent a Four-Wheel-Drive Vehicle to Explore the Local Forests, 61

Bike through Town on a Brewery Tour, 4

Enjoy a Leisurely Walk around an Alpine Lake, 70

Cruise the Sights along Old Fall River Road, 80

Explore Rocky Mountain National Park on an Open-Air Jeep Tour, 60

Watch Sunrise from Centennial Open Space at Knoll-Willows, 83

• •

Bighorn sheep

INDEX